RAMEY HOUSE PUBLISHING

Got Five!
A System For Growing

Created and Written By
Kirsten D. Person Ramey, Ed.D., LPC
2014

Copyright © 2014 Kirsten D. Person-Ramey

All rights reserved.

Kirsten D. Person-Ramey, Ed.D., LPC

ISBN: 0692249710
**ISBN-13:978-0692249710
(Ramey House Publishing)**

DEDICATION

To my mother and father, Shirley and Auther "Joe" Person for helping me make good decisions and to my children Amaris, Aria, Anais, and Aliya for trusting me to help them make good decisions. To my siblings-thank you for allowing me to be such a big part of your children's lives. Lastly to my husband, Rev Roc Ramey, thank you for traveling this parenting journey with me!

CONTENTS

Acknowledgments	I
Introduction	1
Step 5: Listening	10
Step 4: Watching	28
Step 3: Smelling	46
Step 2: Touching	64
Step 1: Tasteful Words	82
Bonus	103
About The Author	116

ACKNOWLEDGMENTS

Without the honest, open, and transparent conversations between the families that I serve and myself, I would not be equipped with the insight to offer feedback and guidance through this handbook. Thank you all for your commitment to build and live emotionally healthy lives by strengthening your families and protecting your children.

INTRODUCTION

When I started my career as a child and adolescent psychotherapist, I have to admit, I did so for selfish reasons. I am a mother and I am an aunt. Both of those roles indicate that I am surrounded by children and often charged with guarding their hearts or at least making sure they stay out of trouble! My goal was to help others, while in the process, help my own family enjoy emotional health as well (or once again, at least help them stay out of trouble). I have always welcomed a challenge, and boy did I encounter one when I decided to service juvenile offenders! During my Master's level practicum experience (much like an internship), I was placed at a transitional center for adult offenders, so I was all too familiar with frank (unsolicited) opinions and bluntness by the time I started working with juvenile offenders. I came to accept "telling it like it is" as a way of life for the offender.

Some of these individuals felt that he or she had nothing to lose, as well as nothing to gain, so why not say the first thing that came to their minds, no matter how rude? I was also privy to the softer sides of these so-called hardened criminals. I say so-called because I have witnessed some melt to tears during sessions about situations that had occurred years ago! Yes I said it, during individual and group sessions, the masks were lifted. I started to see their human sides and this challenged me to learn even more about the concept of rehabilitation. "How do people get better," I asked myself. I hate to be the bearer of bad news and suggest that it is not by lifting weights and reading every book in the prison library. While those activities may make one stronger or smarter, that is not ultimately how people get better.

In working with adult offenders and subsequently juvenile offenders, I started to recognize unique patterns. Regardless of their origins, these offenders ended up with the same fate and furthermore, they had even decided to take similar paths to get there. By retracing the steps of the offenders, I learned that if I could understand their journey towards incarceration, I could create an alternate route, with a willing traveler of course. I quickly started to discover that there are signs that we as parents, grandparents, aunts, uncles, mentors, teachers, neighbors, and counselors can recognize and address to decrease the likelihood for rehabilitation. Instead, we could focus on prevention. It was at this very moment that I abandoned the thought of creating theories to argue with those "strong, smart offenders" who would bet everything on their books that they had been successfully rehabilitated. That was a battle that I would never win anyway. Instead I started to focus all of my efforts on learning about prevention. My new question became, "how do people avoid the need for rehabilitation?" All signs pointed to prevention.

It literally hurts my heart to sit in the living room with a parent so used to a judge (who oftentimes has just met the juvenile offender) giving direction, that the parent has no idea about how to create his or her own judgments about parenting. This is by no means a slight to the many judges whom I have a great deal of respect for. Parents must be empowered to formulate their own goals for the purposes of rearing productive citizens.

In practicing prevention, we use our five senses in order to address our children in meaningful ways that can impact their lifetimes. I share practical tips with you in this guide and while I do not guarantee that your child will never spend a day in jail, I am confident that when practiced consistently, the 6 steps here can empower our children to make wise behavioral choices. It is never too early to start thinking about and actually providing an environment where children cannot only survive, but thrive as well. I have seen children as young as four with extreme behavioral problems come into my office. I simply ease their parent's overwhelming fears by reminding them "he's been here for forty-eight (48) months versus our collective half a decade or more, we have wisdom and experience on our side." While the parent may have lost all sense of patience and sanity (or so it seems), my reminder lessens the frustration a bit. I do this to empower the parent. Believing change is possible, leads to pro-social action towards that change and that is more than half of the battle.

I must pause here to state something that I took for granted, but you may not have thought about as you may be in the process of putting this book down....This book is intended for EVERYONE and is not exclusively for those who have children with legal backgrounds. While some parents may have children who could be poster children for the Department of Juvenile Justice, others may have innocent little nine year olds who arbitrarily smack girls on their backsides and are suddenly introduced to the world of DJJ! Trust me, while I am not attempting to scare anyone into buying this book, it is a lot easier for children to be introduced to the world of Juvenile Justice than some parents may care to think. Whether you have an obnoxious three year old (trust me I feel your pain), you're the aunt of a troubled ten year old boy, the mentor for a fifteen year old girl, or you work in a daycare, you need this guide. It only becomes too late when your child enters the adult prison system. In those cases, precious childhood is lost, but rehabilitation may be the answer towards a life of purpose and meaning. I know what you're thinking, "she's worked with lots of kids in trouble with the law; my kid isn't, so this book is not for me!" Within this handbook, I will constantly talk about the juvenile justice system because I want to make it clear that I don't want your child to go there! This handbook is about parenting choices. It's for anyone who has a kid because I have seen them all; from those in subsidized housing to those who live in cities described as "highly affluent."

Let me be clear about what this handbook intends to do and what I am purposefully straying away from. I intend to be your guide in this process, but by no means am I suggesting how you are to ultimately raise your children. I am a parent so I can imagine how humiliating it would be for some "expert" to belittle my parenting methods by suggesting that theirs are superior. As a counselor, a therapist, and an advocate for our population of children, adolescents, and young adults between the ages of 8-19, I desire to share with you through case examples and personal experiences. Of course names and situations have been altered to protect my clients as well as to ensure my professional integrity, although some of my clients have begged to have their names and experiences included (go figure). Through my examples you will be able to understand how to make minor and at times more extensive adjustments to the way in which you approach the children in your life.

I will say to you what I say to my parents in private practice; take what you will from the things that I say. I am simply the messenger, but I don't beat anyone over the head with my message. I made a decision early on that I would make a commitment to the young people at my job, within the community, but most importantly, within my home. I won't bore you with statistics, but the fact of the matter is, there are shocking numbers of children within the juvenile justice system and some are rapidly making their way towards the adult prison system bright eyed and bushy tailed. Even without the numbers, that should scare anyone who has a child as a significant member in his or her life, or anyone who even likes children for that matter. It should scare us all into action!

This guide is based on the accounts of facts, rooted in personal experience. My goal is not to exhibit some all-knowing intelligence or leave you hanging with theoretical jargon. We're all adults here. You can read the letters behind my name and figure out that I'm pretty smart, I don't need to bore you with my intelligence. My goal is to help you, help your child and I am humbled that you are willing to go on this journey with me. I chose the five senses in addition to common sense because we can use them to learn important lessons about the world around us.

I was a home school mom for seven years before I enrolled three out of four of my children into the public school system. I remember like it was yesterday, teaching my then four-year-old, Amaris, how to observe and learn from her world using her five senses along with common sense. When I decided to write this book, it was only after I had applied my own suggestions for understanding the unique world of young people to my own children and the children around me. It was not enough to be a great counselor; I had to deliberately practice being a great parent! Can I get an amen on how hard that can be? I have degrees in psychology and counseling, but parenting comes with no books and study materials at all…or so I thought. Her father (my wonderful husband, Roc) asked this same child years later, how we learn about animals and she simply stated "by studying them and understanding the world that they live in." She spoke volumes, because this is what we must do as responsible adults who love children; study them and understand the world in which they live. I use the example of animals because we as humans cannot readily communicate with animals. This resembles communication breakdowns between adults and children. We often speculate because most of us as adults have no idea how to speak the language of children and teens. When we are willing to study them, thus begins our own education towards enhancing and positively shaping their lives.

I once told a grandmother that I have no idea how I learned to speak the language of teenagers. I don't know if I simply never forgot it, or if God in his grace simply breathed new life in me as I accepted the call to serve this population. At any rate, I don't take it lightly and I will continue to use that language for as long as I can. The good news is, I will share some of that insight that I have learned with you.

Our children live in a society in which they are bombarded with messages on a consistent basis. I co-own a film company and most of my friends are in the music business, so I realize how influential some of my peers can be in their creative endeavors. It is up to responsible adults who parent children to ensure that the messages they hear from us are used to grow them productively. I have found that it is quite easier to practice prevention, rather than relying on rehabilitation. I am not suggesting that the task is easy, but the differences between the two approaches are significant. It is a lot less overwhelming to apply the principles in this guide, as opposed to talking to your teenaged son behind a glass.

Why would I write such a guide you might ask? I get PAID to service juvenile offenders, so working to prevent or at least decrease the juvenile offender population seems counterproductive to what I spent so many years in school for. Actually, I feel quite the opposite. In truth, I would much rather make a living by educating parents. Although it has become quite natural for me to perform community based counseling sessions within the home, it still gives me chills to sit at someone's dining room table and teach coping mechanisms when their child has been committed to the state. I applaud you for not giving up on our most precious assets and wish you well on your journey of practicing prevention.

So, why the five senses, you might ask? In reflecting on my work and paying careful attention to the way that I develop and maintain my relationship with my own children, I have started to realize and accept some very basic truths. Children want to be listened to, supported, understood, appreciated, and validated. Coincidentally or maybe purposefully the five senses can be utilized in such a manner to help them successfully reach those meaningful life goals. My husband is an ordained minister, but I promise you, I won't suggest that you "pray your problems away." Regardless of your personal beliefs, I'm here to help you learn how to use practical applications to your own parenting journey. That's it! No hidden agenda. I want you to thrive as parents! I want your children and teens to trust your parenting plan. Thank you for allowing me to be a small part of your success.

5

Step 5: Listening (Hearing)

Listen. I could have ended the chapter here and called it a day, but the truth of the matter is, most of us adults have no idea how to listen to the silent tears of children and adolescents. Don't worry, this skill can be learned, but it requires a generous amount of effort on the part of a caring and concerned adult. I remember reviewing session tapes in which a colleague of mine consistently dominated her therapy/counseling sessions. She talked about 90% of the time, in comparison to her client's 10% talk time. She clearly wasn't listening because her client wasn't even getting a chance to talk.

My problem was different. I didn't dominate conversations, but I wasn't exactly listening either. I was simply anticipating what the speaker would say next to make sure I had a wise and clever response. Sound familiar?

At times when we speak to the young people in our lives, we have an answer for them regardless of what their response will be. You can only imagine the surprise I got when a client talked for forty-five minutes straight. That is the day I learned the lesson that I am sharing with you, and I have a 15-year-old African American boy to thank for that!

Many times as adults we don't listen because we believe that we have all of the answers. That couldn't be further from the truth. Yes, we have experience on our sides, but many times it is impossible for us to have all of the answers when we don't know any of the questions. Parents are often amazed at how quickly their resistant teens open up in my office; some parents are even resentful because they do not understand how a stranger can influence their child to speak when their teen walks around the home in silence.

In some cases, parents assume that it is my role as a therapist that influences the child to speak. This may or may not be true. I hear horror stories from clients and colleagues alike about how some young clients go to great lengths to avoid their therapists. Anything from guarded body language, hiding under chairs, or even running away is fair game in the client's opinion. These behaviors are not just reserved for young clients. I had a 17 year old girl explain to me how she hid under a desk every time her counselor came to visit her at her group home. I don't know what surprised me most; her age or the fact that she was five foot nine.

Some kids just don't like therapists because they don't want to be viewed as "crazy." Others don't like the term "counselor" because it is synonymous with school somehow. I simply combat this disdain for clinicians by saying "call me what you want as long as it is not a five letter word." It takes some a minute or two to get that one.

I want to let you in on a little secret here. I am met with three responses to my presence in the room. The first response is general compliance. This is either because they have poor boundaries and cannot wait to talk about their lives; they have good boundaries and recognize the benefits of counseling/therapy; or they are intimated somehow by the differential in power once inside of the therapy room. The second response is complaining, as a result of past situations in which "boring counselors" asked the ever so-popular question…."how are you feeling," and the last and "favorite" response is silence.

The first response, general compliance delights me. I can find out so much about these young people personality wise by how they approach this compliance. If they have poor boundaries and are eagerly willing to engage, it says a lot about their social world. Of course some children just like to talk, but when children are excessively loquacious and willing to share with strangers, it usually suggests some unmet need. The need for authentic care and concern may be missing from their perception of their social world. Remember parents/caregivers, in the life of a young person, perception is reality. Just because you care deeply for these kids does not mean they "get" or accept your messages of care and concern.

Excessive compliance may also be indicative of underlying problems with their interpersonal relationships. When this is the case, the boundaries usually extend to the physical realm as well. For instance, I once had a client who insisted on sharing her life story with me from day one. She was a "touchy feely" type of person and though I am as well with my own children, I am careful not to cross that line with clients. After further exploration, I found that she had a history of neglect and sexual abuse. She wasn't just a kid who liked to talk, she needed to talk and she would talk to anyone who would listen. So what does this imply for parenting? Well, if a child is unusually open to the prospect of talking to others, yet as the parent, you are in the dark on most aspects of his or her life.....a red flag should go up, fast, quick, and in a hurry. Something is going on and it is up to you to find out what it is.

The young people who talk because they are intimidated usually lie. This is true whether or not they are sitting in front of a counselor or a parent. When kids feel inferior, one way to boost their esteem is to create. I once had a client who supposedly told his father everything....everything he wanted to hear! In both of my roles as a parent and as a counselor, my ultimate goal is not to engage in full fledged detective work, although I must rely on those skills (and I will mention them later in this guide).

I once had a supervisor who informed me, "it's not your job to find out if they are lying or not." I beg to differ. As a counselor, I work hard to establish an environment of trust and understanding because if the entire relationship is based on a lie, I am only being manipulated by the individual that I seek to serve. A colleague of mine was led astray for about four months before she stopped trying to be a friend and instead became the counselor she was educated as.

Sometimes as parents, we just want an answer and that is just what we get. Young people have no problem creating worlds for us if we are willing to believe those worlds. I know you're thinking, "there is no way to ensure that a kid will always give you the truth," and you're absolutely right, but if the adult(s) establishes a "safe" environment, there is a greater chance that the young person will engage in truthful exploration of his or her problems rather than just telling us "something." I once had a parent tell me, "She just tells me something so I will shut up." Our kids should not feel pressured to create fictional tales for us so they can share their thoughts. I suggested that the mother quiet herself for a moment and she was amazed by this novel idea. By being quiet, we give our children the opportunity to safely explore their own feelings without having to always hear our two cents. Yeah, I know that was a hard one to swallow, but parents sometimes we just talk entirely too much!

One reason that we as parents do not naturally create safe places for communicating is because we may not fully understand the importance of bringing a kid to a level playing ground. When I am disturbed by something my children have done, I tend to show my anger. I will admit to you, if I was enrolled, I could have possibly failed anger management a couple of times. It's the old AA principle, I can teach you because I know. I have lived it! Kids pick up on this anger, so I usually remove myself from the room that I am in and I go to another room. I chew a piece of gum or eat a piece of candy because in a strange way, it calms me and allows my mouth to engage in an activity other than frowning or screaming to the top of my lungs. I often laugh when I think of the day that I took this practice of giving my mouth another activity other than frowning to work with me. I ate 15 peppermints! Not only did I not show my frustration, but I also had the freshest breath in the office.

Once I am centered enough to engage them, I invite my children back into the situation. This takes practice, but it helps. Sometimes, I suggest that the child go into the room first, but in both situations, it gives the parent time to simmer down one's nerves. Calming down is extremely important because young people do not like to talk when things are heated. They scream and we as adults usually lose our objectivity. This is not the ideal environment to successfully listen to your child's concerns.

Provide an environment of balance and a young person will feel respected and heard. When there is chaos, they know what to expect...more chaos. If the conversation is deliberate (on the part of the adult) and mutually respectful, there will be no urgency to create and perform anti-socially. In a chaotic environment, my eldest daughter creates ridiculous accounts of truth. Ironically in a stable and balanced environment, she talks and I listen. She talks about the hard things and I listen. She even criticizes (respectfully) and I listen. This is the point in which we as the adults have to be mature because when they are willing to talk, we have the opportunity to gather important information from our children. I have found that even if they know that they will suffer some type of adverse consequence, if given a true listening ear, young people will talk.

I recall "Danny," a 13-year old male in the Juvenile Justice System. He had lost both his mother and father to AIDS and was living in a foster home. His only sense of family were his gang members and one uncle whom he maintained contact with. During our last session, he described rules and regulations that he had purposefully violated and gave detailed accounts of his activities outside of the foster home. He recognized that some of his actions were reportable and when asked why he decided to disclose the information, knowing that, he simply replied "because you care." Had I been like most of the people in his life who saw him as a legal charge, he probably would not have shared that information with me.

There is power in showing someone respect by listening to them. The listener is in essence saying to the speaker, "I value what you are saying. I value you." Those words are especially powerful to a young person. It is not that he suddenly forgot that all of his actions could get him in a great deal of trouble; he trusted that he had shared his feelings with a safe person. Ironically, he reported his actions to the proper authorities himself.

At times, when a kid gets incarcerated, the first person that they blame is a loved one. "You didn't do x, y, and z so I ran amuck." It amazes these loved ones because before the incarceration, the kid didn't even talk much about his or her problems. Part of their declaration is old fashioned manipulation rooted in their inability (or perhaps unwillingness) to take responsibility. For the most part, when a kid says this, what he or she means is simple. "We did not respectfully dialogue about the expectations of life. I did not talk to you because I did not know how. I knew how to talk to my antisocial friends, rob people, and commit crimes. That is what I knew how to do, but respectfully communicating with you is something that I did not learn because it wasn't modeled." Parents, you will probably never hear those words or anything remotely like them, but trust me....I have heard a paraphrase of the aforementioned, dozens of times!

In private practice and in the community I have one rule....mutual respect. Scores of children and teenagers have heard me say time and time again...."I respect you and you respect me." This is ironic news to some, but I don't naturally expect children to respect me simply because I am an adult. So many adults lie to children, disappoint them, abuse them, and sexually molest them. These are not just the experiences of those living in group homes and foster care. Children from so-called regular homes are abused and belittled by parents, teachers, coaches, neighbors, random strangers, and even Sunday school teachers each day. With this being said, why should they respect me? For all they know I can be just another adult with poor boundaries planning to hurt them. My job is to restore the confidence in adults that has naturally been dissolved over time. I do that by respecting their boundaries, their experiences, and their right to reveal their story in their own time and in their own way.

Silence is interesting to me. Both as a counselor and as a parent, I used to view it as the ultimate slap in the face. Counselors get paid for the successful communication towards emotional health that is shared with a client. There are seminars about the implications, fears, and even benefits of silence. I now view silence as an opportunity. If your child never speaks to you, that is an opportunity to reconstruct the relationship as a whole. Yes, teens are often in a world of their own, but your teen should not live as some hermit, carefully hiding out in his or her own world, leaving you as the adult to wonder who and what is a part of that world. I use a young person's silence to my advantage.

I used to believe that during times of silence, the answer was for me to talk. At times, that may be right, but most of the time, it is time for me to actually listen to what the silence means. This takes practice because you have to get to know your child. Just as a new mother has to learn what each cry from her newborn means, we have to learn the language of silence. When working, this can be frustrating with a new client. I do not know him or her, so I have to rely on the consistency of human nature to be my guide….what would a kid I know be feeling in this situation? This can be difficult to size a kid up within a matter of moments but I must do it each day. Parents you have the advantage in knowing your child from the womb. Why not capitalize on that advantage?

My four daughters are all different and I am careful to figure out if they are silent because of frustration, anger, disappointment, or fear. These underlying reasons will determine how I react to the silence. When frustration is present, I attempt to reduce it by exploring what is triggering the frustration. When anger is the culprit, the main objective is to reduce the anger. I suggest never engaging another individual when both parties are angry. It is a fruitless effort because the only thing that can happen is a power struggle. Getting involved in a power struggle with a child or teen is the worst thing that an adult who wants to be taken seriously by the child or teen can do. Power struggles dumb the adult down to simply being a bully. Yeah I know it hurts, it hurt me to when I realized that I had bullied a couple of kids.

I always tell my children that they have a right to become angry, but never disrespectful, so they realize that they have parameters in which to express themselves. I do not engage them when I am angry because it will get me nowhere. I must pause here to admit that at times I want to, but their father cautions me. He is the calm one. I often joke that he can keep a cool head in the midst of a hurricane. Not me. I had to learn this skill over and over again. Have you ever heard of the phrase "practice makes perfect?" Well I am still working on it. I used to think, "How can I discipline when I am not angry?" It is quite easy once it is put into practice. The lessons are more concrete to my kids and they take ownership and responsibility for their actions because I can process my decisions and even engage them, rather than exploding and grounding them for a year! If a child is disappointed, he or she needs nurturing and you just can't offer much nurturing when you are actively angry.

Lastly, when fear is present, the response should not be the same as that for frustration or anger. The fear needs to be reduced through addressing it and working together to overcome it. This is what it means to listen to the silent tears of our children. We can learn so much from their silence, but it is only when we start to listen and understand them when they actually start to speak with words that we just might understand. The key here is to reduce frustration, fear or anger to successfully open up the lines of communication.

Now it's time to learn some quick therapy techniques for home use. Body language is paramount when communicating with our children. Eye contact, head nods, and smiles are all involved in what we call engaged listening. When someone is engaged, they are committed to what is taking place. Our children specialize in whether or not we care anything about what they are saying to us. Of course I am not suggesting that one should smile in the face of tragedy, but the goal here is to communicate with our children not only when things are hard, but also in times in which laughter and happiness is warranted. I once had a client who would say the most obscure statements and then look at his mother's reactions. She would usually frown when he explored his abnormal fantasies which may have been a form of manipulation, knowing him like I do. At any rate, he looked to her for her validation. At some point, I just couldn't take it anymore. I use mirror exercises with my clients and I suggested that this mother use mirror exercises for a different purpose; to look at her own facial expressions. She was assigned this task for a week (until our next session). My goal was not to have her evolve into some conceited individual, but I wanted her to reflect on some of the things that her son said and then purposely notice her facial expressions. She was stunned by what she saw when she detected her own expressions. I can only imagine what he had been feeling watching his mother frown at him for some three months.

Some people do not like eye contact. It is viewed as an intimidation technique, but if an adult uses appropriate eye contact, meaning he or she is not attempting to bore a hole in the child's soul; young people feel validated. By using one's face and body language to show interest, the mood is lightened and young people share more. The main objective here is moderation. Too many head nods and smiles come across as fake. The goal is to show a genuine interest in what they actually have to say. When my daughters speak, I am careful not to interrupt either one of them (even if my sweet little Anais takes an hour and a half to recall a five minute story).

You can even go so far as saying that we have rules of engagement. Some say that folded arms seem to indicate a closed mind, but I have learned through the years how to use folded arms in union with appropriate eye contact to symbolize that I am carefully processing everything that is being communicated to me. I think it is important for parents to know their own bodies well enough to come up with their own unique styles for successfully engaging their kids. My older brother has this thing that he does in which he gently pulls his cheek as someone talks. While this may be a simple nervous condition, I convinced myself as a small child that this gesture indicated a deep interest in what I had to say. Once again perception goes a long way. We know that our body language is perceived in a positive light when kids consistently open up to us.

When we can show young people that we value what they are saying through empathetic listening we increase the chances that they will continue to share with us. Once they see that it is not so bad, they may even come to us BEFORE they make a mistake. A major point that I try to share with parents and caregivers is that each word that leaves his or her mouth should be purposeful. Let me help you understand what I mean. At times, we (me included) have said the most non-productive things to our children out of anger. Out of frustration, we threaten to send them to an absent parent (whom we know will not accept the responsibility of raising them), we belittle them, we break their spirits. The goal is to work out our own problems on our own so that they (our issues) do not interfere with our ability to successfully parent. Our children should not be burdened with our negative energy. That is for us to handle outside of the parent-child relationship and possibly through our own therapeutic relationship with our own individual counselor or psychotherapist.

Another major technique to use is reflective listening. When we are able to reflect back to our children what they have said to us, we empower them. When they hear their words reflected back to them, they know they have a listening ear. My second child Aria is often the poster child for "the Middle Child Syndrome." Although I have four children, she represents the title of middle child well. Even if I were to spend 23 hours straight with her, if I dose off during the last hour of the evening, she will feel a sense of neglect. Of course, I am exaggerating here, but only to bring home my point. When she tells me a story, I am fully engaged. I reflect to her everything she has shared with me so she feels a sense of safety and understanding.

One day, that will come in handy because she may have some hard topic to share with me, but the fact that I value her words will resonate within and the pressure to communicate will dissolve. We set ourselves up for how we will deal with challenges, based on the way in which we deal with the good times. I suggest practicing spending at least 15 minutes of uninterrupted time with each child each day, just listening to what they have to share. In my home, at times these conversations range from school issues, to plans for the future. These "talks" should not seem forced, instead they should become a regular part of one's day. Regardless of how tired I am, I set aside precious time for my children.

When I pick them up from school, I ask them about their day and I get an earful. There is never a dull moment in the Ramey Family car! I laugh, I smile, I nod...I listen. The cool thing is, my eldest daughter automatically tells me about her day because that is the practice we have set up. Unlike some of her peers, she knows that her parents have time for her because we make it very clear to her that while work pays our bills, it never comes before the welfare and heart issues of our children. You will never find me on the phone listening to the latest gossip, while ignoring the needs of my children. I actually took a year off from work once, simply because my children needed extra support from me. After that, I vowed to only work for myself because my job was too overwhelming otherwise.

Our children deserve our listening ears (both of them) more than anyone. When our children really need to share heart issues, it is not the time to multi-task. I am not suggesting that we abandon all responsibilities and cater to our children twenty-four hours of a day, but we must be careful to communicate with them on a daily basis. Many parents lose their children to the American prison system, depression and even death each year. Why be faced with such a situation before you take the need to communicate seriously? Whether they use words or not, our children are speaking each day, but are we sensitive enough to their needs to actually listen? I often tell parents that if they are "willing to listen to anything, children will tell them everything." Listening to the stories that do not seem so important at the time somehow build a bridge of safety so our children will talk to us about their innermost thoughts.

I once saw a mother who complained that her 17 year old son never opened up to her about anything. The problem is, when he did talk, she would cut him off and argue with him over the smallest details. Although many times her interruptions were rooted in the fact that he was lying or perhaps stretching the truth, she was doing a great deal of relationship damage by not giving him the freedom to talk. Had she confronted his prevarications after he had a chance to express himself, she would be privy to the internal thought pattern of her child. Now some may argue that it is a waste of time to allow children to engage in fanciful storytelling, but I respectfully disagree. We as parents and those who care about children can learn a great deal from the things that children say. While it is no secret that liars continue to walk the face of the earth, it is noteworthy to mention that children perceive the world differently than their adult counterparts. When we take the time to listen to their views, we are afforded with vital knowledge about them.

Learning to listen effectively is an art and a science and so is raising children. We as parents have to constantly learn new ways to effectively engage our children and though there may be tried and tested methods of childrearing, things change. Long gone are the days that most parents hold tightly to the belief that children should be seen and not heard. I do believe there was once merit to such thinking but in today's Western culture, we cannot afford for our children to remain silent. They see too much. They are exposed to so much that they need an outlet to verbalize their feelings. I would much rather a caring and trustworthy parent to be that outlet instead of a perverted individual looking for a good time at the child's expense or an anti-social peer with nothing to lose. By allowing my children to respectfully verbalize their thoughts, I do not lose power in the parent-child relationship, I gain understanding. My children trust me because they know I will listen to their concerns. Although I will not agree with everything that they may have to say, as long as it is said in reverence, I have no qualms. With a willing attitude to listen, children WILL talk. I would not say it if I had not personally/professionally witnessed this phenomenon time and time again.

4

Step 4: Watching (Seeing)

We see exactly what we want to see. I say this often to parents who insist that there were no visual signs whatsoever that their child was headed down the wrong path. I am not saying that we as parents want our children to fail, I am saying that sometimes we want them to succeed so bad that we ignore when they are failing. I can't tell you how many times I hear "Oh, he's fine," when a child is clearly engaging in behavior that leads to the one way street of destruction. These "fine" parents with "fine" kids are not limited to those that I meet out in the real world. Many of them make their way to my office, and I can't help but wonder if they are so "fine," why they are there in the first place.

It takes a certain degree of vulnerability to reach out for and actually accept help, but I have found that parents must be honest with themselves. I liken it to going to a medical doctor with chest pains. The patient complains and when the doctor suggests the necessary tests to determine if the individual is experiencing a heart attack, the patient suddenly states that the pains are no big deal. As a psychotherapist and a parent I would rather err on the side of believing everything to be a crisis rather than losing just one child to the juvenile justice system.

I once had a client whose young son was experiencing some major psychotic behavior. I believe if given the chance, I could write an entire book about his symptomology. The child confided in me rather quickly and his case though confusing, was not impossible to conceptualize and treat. The mother, like many mothers that I have seen decided that she would no longer bring him in for sessions after I saw him three or four times. While I do not claim to be the best therapist that ever practiced, I am confident that I did nothing unethical, immoral, or disrespectful to help her make that decision. It was clear; she was not ready to accept some of the things that she would eventually find out if she had stayed in therapy with her son.

Some parents choose to come to a couple of sessions, but they don't yet have the strength to go the distance. Often in therapy things get worse before they get better. The very act of processing some of the harsh realities of a client's life can be overwhelming, but the outcome can be promising. The problem is, some people can't deal with the "hard parts" in order to get to emotional health. Parents close their eyes to obvious truth. I have to admit, as a therapist this frustrates me and as a parent is frightens me.

I cannot fathom why anyone in their right mind would turn a blind eye to the emotional turmoil that some children face on a daily basis. If a medical doctor suggested to a parent that a child had a grapefruit sized tumor growing in their brain, I cannot imagine that a normally functioning parent would respond by refusing to accept the news and pledging to never go to the doctor again. I realize that there are some parents that may experience a brief period of denial or due to religious convictions, rely on spirituality in this situation. Even within a spiritual approach, most parents would still address the medical situation.

The thing about mental health and emotions is that we cannot readily see the turmoil that is caused. An MRI, EKG, or CAT scan cannot be used to show many of the important aspects of mental health. While there are some measures that can determine chemical imbalances in the brain, for the most part, we must rely on the subjective experiences of the client to fully understand what he or she is experiencing. Due to this fact, at times we in the mental health field are at a disadvantage. We must look at behaviors in order to help us understand presenting problems.

If your child is acting out, rather than focus simply on the behavior it is essential to look beyond the behavior to understand the hidden language of your child. I am by no means suggesting that parents should never discipline children. I am actually suggesting the exact opposite. Discipline is essential, but it takes place long before a problem evolves. Children learn discipline when disciplined behavior is first modeled by parents. It is important to remember that depressed behavior, negative behavior, and unacceptable behavior in general is typically only the visual manifestation of the actual problem. When we watch for the signs we can understand if this poor behavior is simply a symptom of a larger problem.

There was a young man, Thomas, who fought for sport. He would fight anyone for seemingly no apparent reason. When I suggested to his mother that she literally keep a log of his fighting, while also redirecting his violent behavior she was somewhat confused. I always suggest journals and logs to parents because number one, it helps them to look for triggers to the poor behavior. The biggest reason that I make this suggestion is that it forces the parent to watch and observe the behavior of his or her children. Depending on how receptive parents are to this log keeping, I learn valuable information about the dynamics of the family.

When parents engage in log keeping, I know that I can rely on them to reinforce what is done in session. I know that they are willing to take the time to turn their child's situation around for the better. When Thomas' mom started to keep the log, she found that many of his angry behaviors were precipitated by interpersonal conflicts in which he was clearly the stronger party. In his life outside of treatment, Thomas had an inferiority complex so fighting was a way to gain a sense of supremacy and even normalcy in his mind.

At first glance, the adults in his life thought that he simply fought everyone, yet in all actuality he was particularly deliberate about the individuals whom he fought with. He was tired of being the victim in his own life so he transferred that role to others. Growing up, people in my neighborhood would refer to kids like Thomas as a "punk," someone who fought less powerful opponents yet shy away from equal or stronger opponents.

In all honesty, many bullies fall under this category; they fight because it gives them a false sense that they have power. As a parent it is important to recognize the signs of a bully and then quickly sow love and compassion into that child so he or she no longer feels the need to act out. Thomas was eventually able to start actually verbalizing his feelings, but only because his mother was willing to engage in step number 5 (listening) coupled with this step (watching).

I had a parent tell me that my one session that I did with her daughter was useless because after the session the child got worse. Mind you, my colleague was out on a sick day and in an effort not to lose the client all together, I saw her as a courtesy to the missing colleague. The intervention that I used with her was simple, but it required monitoring from her mother. I pride myself on using homework assignments and interactive worksheets because I believe that I am only the catalyst to bring about change. The parents are the real change agents. Several weeks after the colleague moved on to another place of employment, I inherited the client as my own. When her mother stated to me that my simple (yet effective) intervention had failed, I immediately followed up with the following...."tell me exactly how you went about initiating the intervention." Of course her response was a blank stare before she burst into tears. Not only had she not been effective in executing the intervention, she didn't even try. She wanted to bring her daughter in for a 45 minute quick fix, but she was not interested in the follow up at home.

While some may think that I am being too harsh, I must pause here and defend myself against those accusations.... (I've been doing this for a while, so I know that some of you are offended). I have four children. I know that parenting is difficult, but I also know that when I turn to help, it is up to me to follow up at home. I use medical examples often because I figure for the most part people respect the medical field. When I have a sick child, I take her to the local urgent care center if it is after hours and their primary physician is not available. If the diagnosis is strep throat, I head to the local pharmacy and fill the prescription of antibiotics and give it to the ill daughter for ten days. I know the routine because I have done it before. I listen to the professional advice of the professional and I follow up. If the follow up is observation, observation is what I do. If I opt not to take the professional advice of the doctor, I don't go back to urgent care and tell the doctor that his methods failed. In reality, the urgent care doctor did not fail my child; if anyone did, it would be me. This handbook may be short, simple, and to the point, but there is a point here. Parents must take control of their own families and refuse to leave their children's success to mere chance.

Most people are aware that therapists, psychologists, and other mental health professionals often use treatment plans to guide the work that is done with a client. A treatment plan is almost like a roadmap that details how services will be rendered. When authoring treatment plans, I take the opportunity to work in a collaborative effort with the parent to decide how to approach treatment. While I can conceptualize my own work, I empower parents to assist me with this task of treatment plan authoring because based on their observations, I can better serve the kids.

By no means do I suggest that parents do the work for me. I can easily write a treatment plan. I was trained to write thorough treatment plans by arguably (in my opinion anyway) one of the best Clinical Psychologists in the metropolitan Atlanta area. However, just as I do not expect them to do my work for me, I do not expect to do their work for them either. When I meet a family, I believe in giving them a crash course in Psychology and Professional Counseling. I lend them my knowledge to empower them. After all, they are the ones charged with raising their children so shouldn't they be privy to a bit of psychological know how themselves? I believe in teaching parents to find meaning in their observations. By knowing what to look for and how to find meaning in the behaviors that they see, parents quickly realize the importance of not discounting what their eyes are telling them about their children.

When I sit down with a parent, I often ask a very simple question that does not always have a simple answer. I ask, "what do you need from me?" Or "how can I help you?" Although they are well aware of the problems that they face they have no clue as to what they actually want. They usually say something to the tune of "I just need help." Then we must process what help looks like to them. I have had clients who had major impairments in family communication, but their perception of their problem had absolutely nothing to do with communication issues.

I find out how parents perceive their problems and balance that against how kids see their problems and then tackle a way to teach them how to communicate those views respectively to one another. To just delve into teaching communication without taking into consideration how the parties view their presenting issues, I am serving my own purpose in treatment. My time with a family is sacred and I don't waste that time with my own agenda; that is the purpose of my own family therapy and self help. As a counselor, I am enhanced by each family that I help but I am not there to meet my own needs. This is why engaging families in the treatment planning process of therapy and counseling is so powerful.

If a mother tells me that her son has anger, we work together to create meaningful goals, objectives, and interventions to tackle his anger, as opposed to me sitting at an isolated desk in the corner of the library racking my brain to find innovative interventions or simply using some cookie cutter format to create a treatment plan. I have had far too many colleagues surprised by my ability to secure signatures on treatment plans, but this is not a difficult task when the plans are created in collaboration.

I want parents to be able to use techniques long after I am out of the picture because the truth of the matter is, their problems may last longer than their authorizations for services. It makes no logical sense to keep someone in a suffering state when an individual has the ability to empower them through self help. I am not threatened by an empowered parent. I realize that I cannot touch the world, but the spirit of my influence can stretch far beyond my own reach. Along with the parent, I look at behaviors and find ways to encourage more adaptive behaviors. Neither I nor parents can do that with closed eyes!

I recall a situation in which my eldest daughter was playing soccer. Now before I became a soccer coach myself, I didn't know much about soccer, but I knew that it did not involve neck rolling and verbal threats. With my own eyes, I watched a situation unfold between my daughter and another young lady, but I found myself engaged in a "her word versus my word" battle with an 8-year-old. To my dismay, the other parent discounted everything that I said simply because her daughter burst into tears when she was "caught."

By the way, at times tears are warranted, but for some kids (primarily girls), tears are used as the ultimate form of manipulation. Crying makes most adults uncomfortable so we as adults usually give in to whatever our children seek because we do not want to see them cry. At any rate, while it is important to validate your child's point of view, even if it differs from that of an adult (yes adults do lie on children from time to time), it is even more important to utilize the "watchful eye approach."

Perhaps it is the background in filmmaking that I have, but I have always been the type of parent who sees "everything." I pay attention to the minor details in life that others ignore. I cannot stress how many times this technique has afforded me the opportunity to "see things" that others simply overlooked. We have to use this watchful eye approach with our children because just as I recognized the incident on the soccer field, I am also able to notice when things are not right with my children, even within our home. How can the average person with no time make time to watch a child's daily activities? First and foremost, no one can or should monitor anyone 24 hours a day unless there is some psychiatric need to do so. What I am referring to is simply making sure that we are visually aware of our children. This will probably be the bluntest thing that I have to say, but it needs to be said. We as parents found time to engage in the extracurricular activities needed to produce these wonderful additions to our families, so we owe it to them to be present in their world.

I once had a parent tell me that she went to every little league game, followed by every middle school game, and high school game that her son ever had. As a single parent, who had escaped an abusive relationship with the boy's biological father, she made the extra effort to raise the money each year for him to play sports (which by the way is a commendable gesture). She made sure he saw her representing in her school colors at each and every game, but what she didn't realize that it wasn't enough for her to be seen by him, she needed to "see" him.

When he started smoking marijuana and associating with known thugs and gang members, she should have been able to notice the visual changes that were taking place within her son. When his grades rapidly started to decline, she should have been able to notice his change in attitude. When he suddenly started to show up at the "wrong place at the wrong time" and receive legal charges for his affiliations, she should have realized that this was probably not just mere coincidence. When she started to see less of his childhood friends and more men who may have gone to grade school with her spending leisure time with her son, red flags should have gone up immediately. Just as she watched him score touchdowns as a child, she should have been able to notice that she was steadily losing her son to the street.

Some people argue that "teens will be teens," and while that may be true, there is a big difference between what is considered normal teenage behavior and behavior that leads to juvenile justice intervention. Of course, the older they get, teens desire their freedom, yet when firm boundaries are established early on, it is difficult to stray away from that. Some parents lack consistency and this lack of consistency may develop into a lack of boundaries. Our children do not rely on us and do not follow our rules because they have seen our inconsistency on a consistent basis. Let me illustrate this to you.

The same football player that eventually turned to the street probably had those same tendencies as a young child. Either as parents, we thought it was "cute" or the behavior was ignored although it fell outside of the parental expectations. When a child knows that we as parents expect "more," yet we continually settle for less, they have no reason to believe in the things that we say. Parents look at me as if I have horns growing from the top of my head when I tell them that I understand why their children do not act in accordance with the expectations that the parents have for them. When we as parents have expectations, yet we consistently accept behaviors that fall below those expectations, our children have no need to strive to meet the expectations. Children, especially teens rarely put in the work of meeting familial expectations when they know that in all reality they do not have to. This problem is not rooted in child behavioral management; this is a parental behavioral management issue. I apologize for the friends, family and strangers whose toes I just stepped on. This concept of parental behavioral management was a difficult one for me as well.

Eyes are important and at the risk of sounding like a jerk, I believe we have two of them for a reason....to actually pay close attention to our world. If this confuses anyone, our children are a vital part of our world. When we are not "watching" our kids, you can bet your entire paycheck that someone else is. There was a little girl, who was about eight or nine and case studies could have been completed on her intelligence. Burdened with issues of her own; her mother had little time to attend to her, and her father had always been emotionally absent. When the little girl's older sister eventually tired of being the "watchful eye," other eyes honed in on her.

When we lose focus on keeping a watchful eye over our children, negativity takes our place in their lives. Anti-social and disrespectful friends "watch out" for them. It's almost like negative peers know exactly whom they can influence. These peers don't waste their time on kids whose parents are involved in their lives and dedicated to their success. They zoom in on the kids whose parents are always working or always fighting. I find myself often making this point to well-to-do parents who naturally assume that this scenario only takes place within low income families in which single moms spend all of their time working or the guardians of the child are consistently fighting.

News flash, there are scores of children who fall in this category, who attend private schools where tuition is more than the average person's paycheck. Antisocial peers seek them out regardless of socioeconomic status. They befriend the kid that no one is watching. Let me point out something, anti-social does not mean that they are somehow "shy" as most people assume. These kids are against societal norms and should represent every sane parent's worst nightmare. Most parents become aware of these anti-social bonds when they one day find that their child would rather bond with the new friend, (that ironically no one in the family seems to know well) than to engage in usual family functions.

Now of course, kids seek independence and want to explore their own identity away from the family, but in these cases, there is a dramatic shift in mood, functioning, and behavior. The kid seems to be becoming someone else and in all actuality, they are in that process. They are transforming right before our very eyes, but will we see it or will we pretend not to?

What most parents don't understand is that just as I suggest to you to watch your kids, we must realize that they are watching us. They watch and study our every move because our actions or lack thereof provides them with information about how to go about conducting life for themselves. Children who watch parents fight learn a great deal about social interaction. Before I can "check" little Aliya, my youngest daughter, on he behavior, I must conceptualize her behavior based on the behavior that she sees every day, particularly from me or her father. It amazes me that we often wonder why our children are out of control, yet we fail them every day by not addressing our own uncontrollable behavior.

I have always been an emotional person and one day that emotion evolved into anger. Now, there is nothing inherently wrong with anger. It is a natural emotion that occurs from time to time. When I feel this naturally occurring emotion mutating to something that is out of control, I have to decide "Is this how I want my children to handle themselves? Do I want them to believe that this is an effective way to handle stress and disappointment?" My focus has to shift to the well being of my children because whether I invite them to or not, they are watching me. All of my children, but particularly little Aliya makes it very clear that she notices my every move. She imitates me so I have to provide her with some good (appropriate) material so her performances do not shame me. When Aliya was younger, my older sister often joked that she was really a grown up disguised as a toddler, based on some of the things that she said and did. Part of this is simply who she innately is and part of it lies within the fact that she continues to watch and imitate, even as a school-aged kid. This watching and imitation starts at a young age and it becomes a part of our children's lives until they get to the point in which they comfortably develop and maintain their own personalities. It is essential to make sure that when they are young we as parents and caretakers provide responsible images to our children.

I once had a mother tell me that she was frustrated with the son's treatment of women. According to mom, he disrespected women, by calling them names, using physical violence against them, and belittling them. I questioned "where would he receive such messages about life?" Can you believe she had not once stopped to think about her past relationships, the boy's strained relationship with his natural father, (who also disrespected women) and his constant exposure to the mistreatment of women in general. People wake up! The things that we are exposed to; the things we see, impact us. Those images affect us. With that being said, we must make sure that the image our children see in us is acceptable so that they may reflect a similar image.

People often ask me real world ways to do that and I offer this. We make time to watch football, the soap operas, the news, our favorite prime time shows, reality tv and movies. Why not watch our children grow into the adults we are working so diligently to help them to become? Why leave their success to chance when we can redirect them in the midst of a fatal mistake and help them get on the right path again? If we are not watching our children, we cannot possibly stop them and say "hey, maybe go this way instead of that way." We will simply have to wait until after they make the mistake, and then try to figure out a course of action. When a kid is headed down the wrong path, it is not the time to bury our heads in denial. A mother once told me that she stated to others that her "weed smoking" son was fine, even when he graduated to meth and lost significant weight and experienced a swift change in noticeable behavior. She overlooked the numerous thefts and other signs that indicated he was headed for trouble (or better yet, already dancing with trouble). She convinced herself and others that he was "fine," and she eventually lost him. The young man never spent one day incarcerated; instead he died and now his younger brother is headed for state commitment.

The mother did not cause her son's death, but could awareness and action driven by that awareness have prevented it....perhaps. I am not here to discuss what could have been. Prevention is about addressing the problem before there ever is one. The mother cannot bring her son back, but she can learn from all of the things she saw with her deceased son and his experiences prior to his death, to help her son who is now headed for trouble.

A father once met with me and explained that he knew none of his son's friends, he knew none of his teachers, and he had no idea of what type of music his son liked. I jokingly asked "Wow, if he came into this room, would you know him?" He laughed, but after we sat there for a while; the sad reality set in...many parents do not even know what their kids' lives look like because they do not truly know their children. We must be a part of their worlds. This is not an option. Our children need to know that they can look to us for direction and guidance; otherwise they will look to negativity. They will look to friends who mean them no good. When they cannot see love and support from us, they will look elsewhere. Whatever you do, do not allow your child to take their eyes off of you and please, do not take your eyes off of them.

3

STEP 3: SMELLING

Most people laugh at this step, but this one was actually the inspiration for the guide. Parents (at least in my day) were always quick to say "I smell a rat," or "there's something fishy going on here." I laughed to myself as a child when I heard these statements because they sounded silly but I get them now. When things do not add up as truth, a strong aroma of disgust overtakes me. This step is my favorite because with it, I do practice those detective skills that I mentioned earlier. My children's father, Roc and I, take turns playing "good cop, bad cop." Considering that I listen to my children and I watch them, I have no problem "investigating the scene." I will explain that further in just a moment.

During her middle school years, our eldest was notorious for coming to us with ideas (usually originated in the mind of one of her friends) that we would have to be deaf, dumb, blind, and crazy to go along with. She knows that we are pretty smart parents, yet she continuously challenged our common sense. All teenagers do this at some point because after a few times on the honor roll, they convince themselves that they are rocket scientists and we as parents possess brains the size of English peas. Instead of engaging in a battle of wits, I suggest simply playing along....you get more valuable information that way. I laugh to myself because now this same child shares helpful insights to her younger sisters and cousins about the importance of having actively honest relationships with parents.

I knew of an older mother who ALWAYS went for the jugular when she engaged in conversation with her son. While she was an expert at watching him, she never listened so there was no surprise on my part when I saw how he deliberately hid information from her. Even a minor indiscretion could prove grounds for mandatory estrangement (or shall I say banishment) from the family in this particular family. Whenever they talked, the mother immediately went off on him; I mean she literally flew off the handle. While this may have worked beautifully with her own children in the 1960's, this 16 year old teenager was her adopted grandson and her methods were totally ineffective (based on her desired goals to have a peaceful home environment). Had she provided him with an opportunity to at least express his ideas, she would gather insight to the way he sees life.

I listen carefully to everything that my children say, reflect on it, clarify if need be, and then I point out all inconsistencies (and ask for the real story). Some see this as a waste of time, but I need a chance to sniff out the scene to gain a better picture of what is REALLY going on. Children lie, even the well behaved ones so parents have to stay a few steps ahead. It could even help if we jog a little.

Back to good cop, bad cop. Although I do realize that many homes are headed by one parent, I firmly believe that when homes are afforded with two parents, it is imperative to work together. In the case of the single (mother in particular) it is essential to have a male figure in the picture to assist with certain aspects of child rearing. Many women do not take this counsel well. This suggestion is met with opposition because I am a married woman who has a very supportive husband, so what do I know? Many of the women that I come into contact with do not have positive male role models for their children, as a result of the American prison system, death, or even plain ole' bitterness because of a relationship gone bad.

I am not suggesting that all people should be married or even that a woman HAS to have a man in her life. I am suggesting that children need both male and female role models to help balance out their developmental growth. This has nothing to do with sex or sexual preference. We live in a world of men and women and our rehearsal for real life takes place in the home. While there are scores of single parents (mothers) who have done remarkable jobs in raising children, I dare to say that there may have been an uncle, family friend, grandfather, neighbor, cousin, or step-father that may have filled a void left by the absentee father. There are also countless fathers who prove to be rather effective, but generally speaking, raising children in isolation is just not a wise idea. Children belong to a larger society that is strengthened by interpersonal bonds with others. Having parenting partners can greatly reduce the amount of stress that falls on just one parent. Even for same sex relationships, it can never harm a child to have additional supports of both genders. At the end of the day, do what works for your family. My job is not to judge. I just don't suggest going on the parenting journey alone because parenting can be overwhelming when you don't have an accountability partner.

There is a saying that two heads are better than one and I believe that. In our family, one can focus on the immediate emotional need of the child while the other can question the validity of the situation. This is a difficult task for one person to do without becoming overwhelmed. I once had a parent tell me that it is difficult to be both objective and subjective at the same time and I agree. When a 15 year old girl is telling her mother that she has recently lost her virginity, our subjective selves see this as a blow to the heart; frustration, anger and disappointment are not far behind. Our objective selves realize that choking some sense into the young girl is not a viable option, so there is an internal battle that takes place in our hearts and minds as parents. As a counselor, I can readily show more objectivity to my clients because while I care for them, I have a warm detachment from their presenting issues as a way of providing ethical service to them. I do not blur boundaries with my clients so I can be objective while parents take a more subjective approach, but there is one problem....my clients do not live with me. I empower parents and loved ones to practice the duality of objectivity/subjectivity amongst the family in my absence.

Even for the parents who once vowed to hate each other, it is important to realize that the emotional health of the child is stronger than their vowed disdain for one another. I have heard several custodial parents state that working in collaboration with the non-custodial parent was not probable, just as several non-custodial parents have sang the same tired melody. I don't have much patience for parents who are too stubborn to see beyond themselves and their own selfish desires to work towards the mental and emotional well being of their children. I do realize that personality differences may exist amongst parents, yet our children should be more important than those differences. I believe that adults should have the maturity to work together for the good of their children. It amazes me that two people can connect on the deepest level of intimacy to produce a child, yet have no motivation to make sure that the child strives towards living a meaningful life.

I offer no specific steps towards accomplishing this goal other than to simply do it. There is no magical formula for realizing that our children are more important than any differences that we share. I realize that some absentee parents may be abusive and cruel and I am by no means suggesting that a parent subject him or herself as well as the children to emotional abuse. In that case, it is better to find a suitable parenting accountability partner. If you happen to be the abuser and somehow decided to read this guide (which is highly unlikely though possible), I suggest you seek your own individual counselor to deal with your issues and then work towards healing your children. In most cases, mere stubbornness is the only factor that keeps one or both parents from working together. I am speaking to this population when I say (very boldly I might add) "get over it and raise your children." While that may sound harsh (and I actually intended it to be), the harsh reality for our children is that they are suffering. They have no one to advocate for them and they are filing into the juvenile justice systems across the nation like cattle going to slaughter. This is not the future that I want for America's children, I am certain that you share this feeling.

So how does playing good cop, bad cop help to reduce the likelihood of juvenile justice involvement that leads to the adult prison system.....simple. Would you rather question your child about his or her behavior, friends, and whereabouts or would you rather wait for an arresting officer to do so? I don't believe that parents should turn their homes into a mini penal system, but I do believe that we need to know our kids better than anyone else. That becomes more and more difficult as they get older, but it should be our first priority. There are some areas that Roc has more knowledge about so he naturally is the objective one; he can ask questions that I may be too upset to ask. Although I call it good cop/bad cop, there is no bad parent in the situation. Both are allowed the freedom to save the child from a life of destruction, but there has to be a balance to doing it, hence good vs. bad.

Call it what you desire, but the truth of the matter is, hearing some things is naturally going to make parents cringe, but we cannot shy away from the hard "stuff." We need details. We need to know what's going on in our kids' hearts and minds because their actions will follow suit. I once attempted to employ the assistance of an uncle in helping his sister address his nephew's issues. He openly explained that he did not think he could help his nephew because he was too far gone. Ironically, and I say this with the utmost sarcasm, the young boy started to get into even more trouble. His uncle's view of him became a self fulfilling revelation. Had he helped his sister in balancing her interventions towards her son, perhaps there would have been real positive change that took place. On the other hand, I had another client whose entire family seemed to play an integral part in his emotional healing. Everyone from his single mother, his grandmother, and his older cousins had a stake in his positive growth. Day in and day out, they made it to various meetings, court hearings, and school visits. What impressed me most about this family is that they never gave up, despite the difficulty of the client's behavior. I realized that they would eventually tire of their proactive engagement in his life, so I used that to remind them that just as they would one day tire of helping him, he just might tire of acting out negatively if it proved to be consistently ineffective.

By consistently ineffective I mean that if the client could understand that his negative behaviors would not deter his family from loving him and working towards a more productive life with him, perhaps he would start to tire of engagement in those negative behaviors. It was a long shot, but we were consistent as a team and the client eventually understood that while he had an entire system believing in him to change, he did not have enough faith in himself to change. His support system eventually motivated him to change. Like literally watching the grass grow, at times this task seemed impossible, but it did eventually happen through persistent love and support. I am a firm believer that children eventually change when there is someone who invests the time in them to help them understand the benefits of change. Even the worst basketball player can score a basket when there is someone on the side rooting them on.

How long must we wait for change, one might ask. Let me clarify, by no means do we sit around and wait. I mentioned the illustration of watching the grass grow, yet a support team (family, counselors and other interested parties) must not casually sit by and wait for the change to take place; the support system must empower, encourage, and unconditionally love the troubled child through his or her metamorphosis of change. What this may look like in the real world is to take an active interest in the child's positive development and quickly put a halt to negative development. This takes time and a lot of energy. I am a firm believer that parenting is not for punks. If it takes a strong individual to raise a child, it takes an even stronger one to help that child avoid jail!

Parents must constantly practice the art of duality. We are parents in every sense of the word, yet we are also proactive detectives. When we engage in proactive behavior, there is little need to rely on reactive behavior. We investigate before a problem even arises, based on hunches. Now, where do these gut feeling hunches come from, one might ask. They come from our own experiences as children and teens. I dare to suggest that more than likely, between oneself and the individual that we have chosen to procreate with, the apple usually doesn't fall far from one of those trees. The first lesson that I learned in grad school was to "know thyself," and I pass this lesson along to parents. If we know ourselves, chances are we have a basic understanding of our children, whether or not we choose to admit it or not. Times change, and our children are exposed to a different world from what a parent may be accustomed to, but certain urges are just passed down from one generation to the next….that is the beauty of life, because it helps us to predict behavior (if we pay attention).

I was a smarty pants as a young kid and every now and again I rely on a bit of sarcasm to get me through a conversation. It is no real surprise to me that each of my children have somewhat of a smart mouth. They are MY children. Some parents like to argue that their children's abnormal behavior is independent of anything that they have ever witnessed themselves, but if we are honest enough we can admit that while our children may take our behaviors to a higher degree, at the core, lies behavior that we are readily familiar with. I watched a mother interact with an angry daughter. The mother questioned her daughter's defiant and aggressive behavior with little insight to the obvious fact that her daughter inherited her anger from her mother, who used expletive language as if her next meal depended on it. She had probably modeled that behavior to her daughter for years yet she was clueless to the fact that her daughter's behavior was an identical reflection of her own behavior. Just as we are usually quick to suggest as kids that we will never say the things that our parents said to us as children to our own children, (yet we find ourselves eventually sounding like recordings of our parents), the truth of the matter is, our children quite possibly developed behaviors similar to ours, warranting those familiar talks.

I see kids all of the time who have learned bad behaviors from their parents, but because the behaviors may not be the exact same, the parents are baffled as to where the behaviors originated. For instance, a certain teenage boy smokes weed on a daily basis and his father who consumes alcohol on a daily basis cannot understand why said teenage boy smokes. Now, there may be other factors that contribute to the boy's weed smoking, but without probing, the boy's father is unlikely to see the similarities in their presenting problems. That example isn't even hard detective work. It's a matter of looking at the parent in the mirror and having just a brief moment of honesty. Now before parents go and get bent out of shape, I am not blaming every problem on parents, because most of us really are doing our best, but when so many children enter the juvenile justice system at such alarming rates, we have to try something a little bit stronger than our best! If I must, as a parent, I will be the prosecutor, judge, and jury before I allow the fate of my children to rest with people that they do not know. My job is to guide them and even if I get on their nerves in the process…..so be it. My job is not to be their friend anyway. By finding out why the behavior is taking place in the first place, we learn a great deal about how to address the behavior.

    I keep stressing behavior because behavior is usually what leads to legal involvement. No one has ever gotten a charge for what he or she thought in their mind. It is only when thought and action marry, that legal action follows. Investigating behavior cannot start when the child is placed in handcuffs. It has to start in the home, within the classrooms, and on a daily basis. When a child does not want to complete a classroom assignment and resorts to acting out, it is imperative that the adult in the situation take a step back to figure out why the child is not willing to participate.

I once did a parental evaluation for a woman that some would consider resistant, but upon talking to her, I found her to be quite engaging. She expressed concern about participating in the evaluation because she could not read well. A colleague had attempted to engage her in the evaluation prior to my participation, to no avail. I listened intently as she likened it to several situations in her grade school years when she felt embarrassed in class and chose to act out to somehow hide her lack of understanding. While classrooms are overcrowded and it may not seem realistic to process why each and every child acts out, I reason that it makes more sense to do that than to spend the extra hours that it takes collectively over time to address poor behavior that comes as a result of such classroom exchanges.

I had a school visit with a client of mine in which the teacher shared that she chooses to ignore behavior that is not detrimental to the emotional, educational, or physical well being of her class, yet she promptly addresses behavior that could prove to be a problem later. She further stated that she would rather take time out to address acting out behavior that may escalate to a full blown disruption of her class. First and foremost, I applauded her for her discernment, realizing that the art to determine when to engage and when to dis-engage is a skill that must be practiced before it is mastered. She takes control over her class because she is willing to take the time to investigate the core of the problem rather than focusing on behavior only. I do understand that teachers have to teach but being able to investigate behavior increases the likelihood that educators will get the opportunity to actually focus a majority of their time on actually educating students.

This same concept can be applied to home. If we think about it, it would not hurt us as parents to simply probe to find out why a child may be resistant to our expectations. Perhaps children do not see these expectations as reasonable or they may think of them as demands. Children have no power in the family because they cannot readily make choices, so the least they can have is a voice. If they feel as if they have no voice….then they inevitably act out (as a way of expressing themselves) and subsequently somehow they get all of the power. By allowing children and teens to respectfully voice their concerns and opinions, we reduce the likelihood that they will act in defiance and shift the power from the parent to the child.

This may be a confusing concept so allow me to illustrate it this way. When children and adolescents act out, it impacts the family unit as a whole, and the child or adolescent then holds the key to when the family may function normally again. This is giving them power when all they wanted in the beginning was a voice; to be heard and respected. When a misunderstood child is not valued enough in the classroom or home to be understood, he or she disrupts the healthy functionality of the entire system. I see parents who are so set in their ways that they see giving children a voice as an act of weakness. This could not be further from the truth. I even give my three year old niece a chance to express her ideas. While I rarely agree with her developmentally selfish ideas, I do give her the opportunity to express herself and this in turn builds confidence in her. She appreciates the opportunity and she readily shows it through compliance. While all children will not comply to expectations just because they have a right to respectfully express themselves, it is likely that for the most part, children will show gratitude for being respected enough to share their thoughts.

Each day I help parents to investigate what their children and adolescents want and how we can reasonably meet them halfway to get them there. Believe it or not, most children don't truly want to engage in antisocial behavior. Instead, there is some unmet need that is being met by their participation in the unruly behavior.

I had a client who explained to me that he stole cars because he felt a rush by being able to successfully move a vehicle from one place to the next. His life was mundane. He needed excitement, so I had to help him explore pro-social options to meeting that need. After much probing, we figured out that it wasn't even the rush, it was the satisfaction he got from the act, specifically starting the car up. When members of his treatment team commented on his love of joy rides, imagine their surprise when I suggested that that was not where his satisfaction came from at all. I love to ask kids what they are good at and believe it or not, this seventeen year old boy was good at cooking. People look at me as if I am insane when I tell them that I encouraged a juvenile delinquent to replace stealing cars with cooking, but the story is true. It took time to get there, but we did! There was some common pleasure that he got from both acts and our task as a team (the client and myself) was to find out what that common pleasure was. He was hands on and loved creating. Had I not probed into his interest, he may not have revealed his interest in cooking. The fact that I was willing to work with him to try to figure out how cooking could be related to stealing cars helped the client realize something that he truly wanted in life.

An easier example is with my boys who have anger. They fight because they need physical contact. I applaud a certain theatrical film and the real life heroes who realized the connection between repressed anger, low self esteem, discipline, and football. Angry young men easily replace the anti-social act of fighting with playing football. It is the strangest phenomenon that this rage somehow evolves into disciplined roughness that is not defined by uncontrolled anger. When we find out what a kid is truly aiming for, I believe we can help him hit the target, thus producing target behavior. This is work, I won't lie. Investigation involves knowing your child's friends, whereabouts, mannerisms, and the like. It is our full time job outside of our full time job, but it is worth every minute spent doing it!

I remember watching one of my favorite movies as a kid. I loved it so much that I often watch it with my own kids and one of my teenaged nieces. In the movie, there is an African American mother whose daughter rejects the fact that she is biracial. She constantly attempted to disown her mother and she even ran away from home, but her mother traveled to find her. She literally tracked her down in a nightclub, where she worked as an adult entertainment dancer. I did not understand her determination when I was younger, but as mother myself now, I wholeheartedly understand her drive. I met a client whose mother was similar to the mother in the movie that I mentioned. The client ran away often and the mother would always find the client without the assistance of the authorities. She would literally canvass the neighborhood, frequent drug infested communities, and stand toe to toe with known thugs all with the goal of finding her child. Now of course, I believe that children must show respect and some common sense at some point. There was no valid reason for the child to constantly run away other than the fact that structured life seemed impossible. The reason that I highlight this family is because the mother saw no reason to give up on her child. She was willing to go the distance even if it meant going it alone. This child had difficulty with expression, yet music came naturally. Once mom found a common ground of understanding through music her "police work" decreased because her child started to remain in the home and work through processing feelings rather than continuing to run away.

I like projective tests because they require the individual who is giving the test to interpret the results of the test. Most notable is probably the Rorschach test which features a variety of inkblots that an individual is asked to describe as something. Those descriptions are given meaning through interpretations by the test giver. This type of work is like projective work. We ask children to explore their interests and then give meaning to how these interests can replace negative behaviors. Once we have this understanding, we can create and use meaningful interventions. This technique can even be used in a paradoxical way. I used running (track) as a way to help a client cease from running from her problems. Initially she was just a fast runner, but when she joined the track team, she learned about the discipline required to run track and this ironically helped her to effectively process her issues rather than run from them because running took on a new purpose in her life. The key here is to be willing to investigate through trial and error. It takes a determined adult to keep a tenacious child or adolescent out of jail.

2

Step 2: Touching

Touch is essential. It is the universal element that lets us know that we are not alone and someone cares. There is a big debate in my field, concerning whether or not to use touch or not. It is difficult to listen to a 13 year old girl explore her feelings about being raped by her father without wanting to hug her and let her know that everything is alright. The problem is, her abuse likely started with a hug. The power of touch is amazing. With just one touch, I was able to get through some of the most difficult moments in my life. My parents literally touched my soul each time they gave me a hug to let me know that everything would be alright.

I remember when I first started seeing kids in DFCS care. Many of them had been abused, oftentimes by the very people who were supposed to be caring for them (and some received a pretty nice per diem to do so I might add). It was no surprise to me that some of these kids had been victimized through inappropriate touch or the absence of touch all together. The shock came when I saw my first private practice patient who fell into the aforementioned category (remember I like to call them clients, but in my workplace I have to go with the norms of the environment). Here sat in front of me, a 13 year old boy who had never been hugged by his father. The father rationalized this by explaining to me that he was not gay. I wondered what could possess a forty something middle class man to say something so absurd. Since when does appropriately hugging one's own child signify a sexual preference? I believe that there is nothing in the world besides physical paralysis that excuses a parent from reaching out and hugging their child!

I have always been the affectionate type so some of this affection had to rub off on my children's father because he grew up in a family that was not as expressively affectionate. The idea of gender roles comes into play here. In Roc's family, there is the general belief that affection was not as important or common because all of the children were male children. In my family of origin on the other hand, four of us are female, while our oldest sibling is the lone male. Let me eradicate this myth for you....males need appropriate touch as well. Whether it be a handshake on a job well done, a fist bump from a cool uncle, or a fully fledged hug from a father, we cannot afford to send the message to our kids that they are not worth an affectionate touch.

While I am not discrediting the paternal side of my children's family, I use the example to illustrate a common myth among those with male children. My own husband had to overcome this, because with four daughters it is impossible to get to the heart of the matter without adopting physical forms of expression in one's communication patterns. At least in my family this is the case. Of course there is absolutely no doubt in my mind about the sincerity of Roc's family of origin, but it is common for parents of males to believe that touch is not just as important as it is to females. It is true that boys may require less physical contact, but the absence of appropriate physical touch in the case of any child is not a wise idea in my professional and common sense opinion. I think we often miss the point and forget to rightfully assume that these non affectionate males will one day grow up and attempt to form meaningful bonds with partners, spouses, and children. Early modeling of affection can be just what the dr. ordered.

As a teenager, I remember there was a male student who was very aggressive. He fought at every chance he could and although most people thought that that was an oddity, I wanted to know why he was so violent....so I asked him. Even as a younger child I was inquisitive, I wanted to understand behavior and I had come to realize that one way to gain knowledge was to seek it through questioning. The student reminded me of students that I had known growing up who seemed to get a rush from physical violence. Being a person who does not naturally like rough physical contact, I was intrigued by their overwhelming sense of aggression. At any rate, eventually the student became comfortable with me.

Looking back, I guess it was my early preparation to become a psychotherapist that made it so appealing to talk to me. He explained that his father was a demanding man who used physical aggression to control the family. Of course he didn't use those words but as I developed as a clinician, I formulated that interpretation. This aggressive modeling through aggressive physical touch seemed commonplace among all of the students that I mentioned earlier.

I recall school visits from parents of the aggressive students in my early educational experience. These parents reminded me of the description that the high school classmate was offering. These parents made no effort (and if they did it was minimal) to model healthy physical touch to their kids. As a result, the kids became angry and aggressive themselves. It is quite simple to model healthy physical touch to one's kid(s). My husband and I are careful to hug, exchange glances, and hold hands purposely in the presence of our kids. We are their models for healthy physical love. As an extension of our love for one another, we are careful to hug them, hold their hands, and give them pats on the back. At times, I still hold my teenagers' hand when we cross the street. Of course I do not have to do that and ironically neither of them are the least bit bothered by it. My children are the envy of some of their peers because it is readily apparent that they are loved. I have no problem showing it physically.

I remember a session with a community client in a group home that I will call "Mike." He had no living relatives and he had been detained in juvenile more than 10 times in his short 14 year old life. As he spoke about his anger that was actually rooted in frustration and sadness he actually contorted his body into a weird figure that initially had me somewhat worried. Any parent who has ever seen an ultrasound picture can identify with the image that I am describing....he resorted to the fetal position. It only took a brief moment for me to realize that he was regressing to a place of safety; he needed to feel the warmth of a loved one's' touch, although he wasn't even readily familiar with what that looked like in his own personal experience. While I did not touch him, I allowed my words to somehow soothe his soul within the moment. Even as an offender, he still needed touch. He needed to feel loved and validated and I had to wonder how long that had been missing from his life.

"Soul touches" are important. These are times when a child is not physically touched, but the adult somehow still manages to let the child know beyond a shadow of a doubt that he is cared for and respected. While soul touches are very much needed in life from time to time, actual touch is needed as well. Bonding is a concept that all new parents hear about the second the umbilical cord is cut. This is a time for the new parents, especially the mother to "get to know her child" through the use of swaddling and physical strokes.

Imagine my frustration when I had to part ways with my firstborn (who was premature), shortly after her early arrival. I was a young mother and I did not know to demand that those first seconds of her life be spent with me before she was whisked away. There were no obvious complications and she scored a remarkable score of 10 on her APGAR, but yet and still she had to be thoroughly examined. I know now after having three more children (and becoming accustomed with procedures) that she could have been afforded twenty seconds to meet the individual who had carried her, sang to her, read to her, and prepared for her birth for seven months.

I was even more distraught as a young psychology student when I read several books about the importance of touch and unmet needs, highlighting that crucial time after birth. Well certainly not to discredit the men and women of my field who paved the way for me to have a career in the profession of counseling, but I must state that bonding is a process that involves more than just hospital interaction. I know of several women who bond with their children within the confines of the hospital, only to make them a third, fifth, or seventh priority once they are back to the real world. This is not to pick on mothers, but I want to make it very clear….while bonding may be initiated at the hospital (or even during pregnancy as I mentioned in my own life), it is important to recognize that bonding is a process.

Touch is a natural part of life and depending on how the touch is presented and perceived, it can prove to be an important factor in a child's development. The focus of this chapter is cultivating good touch that produces healthy self esteem in order to combat anti-social and negativistic behavior, but I will also share the impact of bad touch as well. I once saw a family and the teenager was autistic. She had an extremely difficult time attempting to settle down. In addition she was diagnosed as having ADHD and she had psychotic symptoms (hallucinations, delusions) as well. My colleagues marveled at my ability to get her focused for 30-45 minutes at a time. What I found most impressive about her situation was her mother's response to her. She stroked her hand as one would do an infant who just couldn't settle down. I watched the young girl's demeanor change from rambunctious and borderline rude-to quiet, peaceful, and cooperative. It literally took less than ten seconds to soothe her, so it irks me to watch a parent casually ignore a child's immediate need for human contact. I do not believe that adults should smoother children with affection on an around the clock basis, but I do believe that sometimes wayward children just need a touch to know that everything will be okay.

I had a client who was being admitted into the hospital and he would not settle down. I suggested his mother simply touch him gently. Mind you, this same young man had recently been very aggressive towards the entire staff and here I was suggesting that his mother comfort him. She looked at me initially with an underlying expression of confusion, but she trusted my judgment and touched her son. Lo and behold, he settled down. What she did (and yes she did it, not me) was to model appropriate touch to him when his first reaction was to be angry and aggressive. When I speak to parents on this matter they often ask, "How can you be so sure in making these suggestions that the aggressive child will not act out?" This will be difficult for some to understand. I honestly do not believe that children and teenagers want to be bad. I think they are simply looking for respect that we as adults don't naturally give them. Since it seems to be the goal of the child or adolescent to be respected in this manner, we as adults must model to them ways to present themselves in such a manner to reach the desired goals. When I get a new client that others deem impossible to serve, I am excited by that challenge. I immediately try to find ways to touch his or her soul because if everyone is afraid of him or her, this probably is missing from the client's life.

I am five foot three and for most of my adult life, I have weighed less than one hundred and twenty-fivepounds so I do not represent a threat to most people. Even as I have gained extra pounds, I am still considered petite by most. Ironically I don't scare easily, so I am not put off by the large sizes of many of the kids that I serve. I describe myself physically to paint a picture. When a woman my size is willing to touch the soul of a young would be, or active offender, I am saying "you are not a monster, you are a precious child." Though he or she may tower over me, I make it clear that aggressive physical contact is not the behavior to be emulated. Now don't get me wrong, regardless of one's physical description, I have a valid point to stress about appropriate touch. For the parent who is bigger than their child, the soul touch response that their touches give is that "I am not too big and powerful to value you." Soul touches and actual physical touch put us on a mutually respectful ground. It is here that appreciation for the child is represented.

In my family, we do a morning prayer each and every morning. We take turns on who will lead it and provided that we are not running late, we go around the circle and all six of us add our individual prayers. While not everyone who reads this handbook will share my exact religious beliefs, the idea here is universal....we touch and agree with our children. This concept can be used for the parent(s) who gives a word of advice each day to the child by giving him or her a hug, or it could simply describe the parent who gives a pat on the back and reminds the child to have a good day. I want my touch to be the last one that my children feel before they go out and face the world each day. There are many temptations out there in the world just waiting for them. If nothing else, I use my touch for them as a shield of protection so to speak. They leave the house each day knowing beyond a shadow of a doubt that they are loved and valued and that belief can confidently compete with any peer pressure that awaits them. Even in my own childhood, I was not perfect, but I did not deviate too far from my parent's expectations because I knew that they loved me and their hold on me was stronger than any touch I could receive from any negative peer.

Children and adolescents are introduced to negative touches in the absence of positive touches. When our kids do not feel a sense of belonging from us, they look for that feeling elsewhere. This could be from a perpetrator, anti-social peers, or even gangs. I am not suggesting that children choose to be victims of perpetrators, yet oftentimes, these individuals seek out children and young people who seem to lack validation.

I once had a female client who frequented chat lines and social networking sites. These environments can be filled with sick individuals looking to negatively exploit young people. So very often when we deal with issues concerning keeping kids away from the Department of Juvenile justice, we fail to acknowledge the fact that some young people are lured into the world of illicit sex each day. This lifestyle often starts in the absence of healthy touch from one's parent(s). While social networks are not inherently negative, sick individuals take advantage of these sites to get to vulnerable victims who may be longing for a touch from someone. Back to my client....she did not have a physically healthy relationship with her mother. Their only physical interaction involved punches and slaps (on both parts). The internet became an escape for the client, who eventually met someone face to face. Luckily she was not victimized by this older gentleman who posed as an innocent friend, but she could have been. I remember educating her and her mother on the dangers of her lifestyle and suggested her mother work harder to first and foremost provide a model for healthy interpersonal interaction and to also physically show her daughter how much she valued her through hugs and the like.

It concerns me that many parents are quick to write the power of physical touch off as something that will not be effective without even trying it. Believe it or not, so many of my clients have reported the reason that they quickly open up to me is because they trust me. My words, but particularly my actions are consistent with the suggestion that I care for them. Parents assume that their children know how much they are loved, while some parents insist on refusing to show them that they do.

Antisocial peers, namely gang and gang-like acquaintances provide something that is missing from a child or adolescent's life. While I do not profess to be a gang guru, I am aware of the fact that most children who are well adjusted in their families or origin, at school, and within the community do not join gangs or other groups that can get them into trouble. I dare to say that there is no reason to, and there is also no time. You know what they say about idle time, well I try to keep my kids busy so there is very little if any time to engage in unproductive activities. I charge each of my girls with the task of stopping their activity at any given point to assess, 1) what they are doing, and 2) why they are doing it. If they don't have a good reason to explain their behavior then most likely it is unproductive behavior. I used to do this assessment for them, until they became mature and responsible enough to self regulate their behavior. I know that there are many parents who may not have the manpower (either because of a single parenting situation or strenuous work hours to ensure that kids are involved in productive activities) or parents who do not have the resources to engage their kids in meaningful activities. This requires some brainstorming on the part of the parent.

When Roc and I started off, we were young and we didn't have much money. We would sign our daughter up for activities, learn as much as we could about the activities and then create our own "free" version of it. We engaged my older sisters in the same task and before we knew it, we had created music classes, play groups, and even clubs to make sure that our children always had something to do. We made our circle so tight, as to avoid negative peer influences that attempted to penetrate what we had going on. In fact, we still do this during a "Purity" group that I developed in 2013. I don't propose that anyone do something that I wouldn't do myself for my own children. I don't believe that finances should keep children from experiencing the life that parents imagine for them. Just because we did not have money in our early years, I did not give in to the belief that my children could not be exposed to activities to reduce their chances of being recruited by anti-social peers. Many may argue that activities cannot keep a child safe from the touch of unhealthy peers. I beg to differ. When a child is touched by positivity in the domains of home, school, and community, there is little room for negativity. The way to build this shield of protection is to first secure the home, build positive and collaborative relationships at school, and to do the same within the community. What is an illustration of that, you might ask....I will delve deeper into that in my next handbook. For now, I will simply state that there must be positive "touches" within the confines of the home, the educational system, and the community. In these cases, the children are less likely to be susceptible to the negativity that can readily embrace them.

As I stated earlier, I am not an expert on the subject of gangs, gang prevention, or gang activity, but I have asked clients from time to time why they opted to join a gang. I am no idiot so I know that many are initiated through physical means. Some may question what would possess someone to be physically initiated into an organization. The answer is simple-acceptance and unconditional positive regard-the very characteristics that responsible parents should be supplying to our kids, yet we often fail terribly at doing so.

There are parents who suggest that they did everything in their power to make sure that their kids refrain from such a life, but I see the issue much differently. A parent can provide love and understanding all day long, yet without deliberately raising a child for success, we still run the risk of losing a hold of our children. In raising my own children, I think of all of the possibilities that could go wrong in their development.

I am not obsessive about this task; I am realistic as I assess the various temptations that await them. After my assessment, I am strategic about putting plans into place to greatly decrease the likelihood of those negative things taking place. I don't want my children being subjected to life in a juvenile detention center where they look to find human contact through fighting. I don't desire to have my daughters engage in illicit activities for the sake of touch and find themselves committed to the state. My goal is not to see my children end up being jumped in or raped into a gang for acceptance. My job, every day of my life is to make them feel secure enough to tackle life on the useful side of life. There is great power in positive touch from a parent!

I often stress to parents the concept of social interest-an Adlerian term that suggest we are all striving to work towards meaning and common good for mankind when we are acting at our optimal best. Before we can effectively contribute to society in meaningful ways, we must learn how to contribute to and be an active member of our own families. We are all connected and this connection may be strengthened through deliberate physical touch that is healthy. I often question parents about who their child is connected to. Many parents do not even know their children's friends. As parents we put ourselves at a disadvantage when we are not certain who our children are connected to. I will put it this way....in the instance of the body, each part works in conjunction with the other. Though it may seem that certain parts may work in isolation, such as the hand to write, other parts of the body are working as well. I will not bore you with the details of how the human body works, but it must be stated that there an alliance among parts. With that being said, who a child and adolescent is connected to as just as important as the individual child. Our connections to others help shape our identity. I cannot stress this enough because these connections are paramount in determining what or who will touch our children's souls.

I once had a client whose mother believed that his environment was responsible for his behavior so she opted to send him away. Many would argue that a move would not result in the young man abandoning his desire for anti-social peers. To an extent, I agree with those individuals but this is a two sided coin. His mother did rightfully acknowledge his connectedness to antisocial peers in his community, but she failed to recognize the missing element in his life that fostered his attraction to antisocial peers in the first place. The young man moved away and while he was positive and pro-social for a time, he eventually identified anti-social peers in his new environment and picked up where he left off. His mother had to then revisit her own interactions with him to figure out where and why she lost him to the touch of negativity.

Often times, parents assume that I am blaming their children's DJJ involvement on them (the parent). In reality, I am calling for action on the part of the parent(s) to actively engage in the life of one's child. I stress the need for the parent(s) to connect with the child and adolescent because it is true that if the parent does not, someone will. It is imperative to fully understand as a parent, who your child connected to and how his or her life is being touched.

I would like to close this chapter with an example. I knew of a mother-not a client, but more like an acquaintance. She had a teenage son. While she showered him with love when he was a small child, she took her hands off of him-literally. She cut off all physical contact because of her disdain for his absentee father, whom the young man yearned to know suddenly when he became a teenager. While this is not uncommon for a child to seek the absentee parent during adolescence (or at least show signs that he or she longs for the parent), this was described as a slap in the fact to the mother who had raised the young man alone to the best of her ability. The two; mother and son grew further and further apart as the young man sought connectedness through his peers. Initially his father was unavailable and eventually his mother became unavailable as well. It was originally emotional detachment, but she eventually withdrew completely. Her son started to engage in minor legal violations that eventually evolved into felonies that resulted in a commitment to the state. As she spoke to him during weekly visits, she longed to hug him for extended periods of time, but this opportunity was not afforded to her. It was against the policy of the facility in which he was detained. After his commitment, he was shipped to a camp that was an extended distance from her home and she was unable to visit him at all. Shortly after he was released from the Department of Juvenile Justice at 17, he was murdered. At his funeral, she leaned down in his casket and kissed him gently on the forehead. I do not feel it at all necessary to provide additional details on why I chose to include this account in the handbook. While the story does not have a happy ending, it is needed to fully demonstrate the point that I am attempting to make with this chapter.

A parent does not fully understand the importance of a hug from a child until that ability is stripped from us. I make sure that I stress to parents all the time that there are two types of glasses that keep us away from hugging our children; the physical glass at many facilities that the offender has to sit behind, and the invisible one that exist right before we lose our children to the juvenile justice system. It is imperative to recognize the invisible glass the moment that it presents itself. When there is an absence of healthy physical touch among the family, it is likely that the invisible glass has already presented itself!

1

Step 1: Tasteful Words

In many cultures and even among various religious beliefs, life as we know it began with a word. To even entertain that hypothesis means that most individuals recognize the power of the spoken word. It is no wonder why I have decided to list this as the final, yet highly important step in working with children to deter them from a life of meaningless existence.

After I had my first daughter, I occupied myself with activities while I was a patient in the hospital. On the outside world, my older (and only) brother was delivering a trial sermon as a minister. Since I would not be able to attend the event, he disclosed the title of the sermon to me. He called it the "Pink Tornado." Of course this was making reference to the tongue and its role in wrecking havoc as well as providing blessings over those in its path so to speak. His thought process was right on point in what I am sharing with you now. With our words, we have the power to steer our children towards the path of greatness or the path of destruction. The sad part is, many of us have no idea of the power that we hold through words. I will shed light on this subject.

In the case of Michael, he hears profane and derogatory language day in and day out in his life, yet his parents show utter surprise when this language becomes a part of his own vernacular. I can't help but wonder is it surprise or shame that leads to their disbelief? As a parent myself, I have come to realize that it is quite illogical to expect our children to develop in ways in which they have not properly been trained. If I curse my child out, how in the world can I rightfully expect her subsequent behavior to be a blessing? His or her behavior will represent the language that has been spoken over them.

Following up from the prior chapter in which I mentioned our daily practice of morning prayer as a way of giving soul touches, it must be added that these touches only work because of the words spoken. These steps are not to be considered in isolation, although I have presented them in this manner. In that respect, I want adults to have a firm understanding of the power of each step, yet an understanding of how they collectively work together for the good of our children. Parents often ask me how the task of "speaking life" over one's child works in everyday life. During my pregnancies, which were all considered high risk for one reason or another, I learned to speak positive statements over the welfare of my children. I had high expectations for each of them, even though there was the possibility that my pregnancies would not end favorably. Although some people warned me not to become too sure of a successful childbirth, I politely tuned them out. I was the one (along with my spouse) who would ultimately be responsible for our children's well being. Although they would eventually be a part of a larger social network, we had to learn to be the children's loudest and most spirited cheerleaders. Of course this bit of knowledge serves the expectant parents well, but what about the parent of a twelve year old who has already shown signs of juvenile delinquency? How does a parent find the words to speak towards the positive development of someone who is not progressing along the useful side of life towards productivity?

I have already explained earlier that children do not innately desire to be bad. Children desire to be heard, supported, understood, appreciated, and validated. It is actually up to us as the adults to help them develop in a healthy manner. It would be insane to suggest that we deprive our children of food, yet so often we are willing to deprive them of social nourishment in the form of social well being, just because we may believe the child is "bad." If a child, adolescent, or teen is developing in an unhealthy way, we must take control of the situation and reintegrate him or her back to the positive and useful side of life. One of the simplest ways to do that is through a positive word. Each time I see a female client, I say "hey sweet girl." While some of my female clients have been fighters, thieves, and downright menaces according to their charts, I choose to refer to them as "sweet." Roc's grandmother's nickname, given by his grandfather was "Sweet," and this is a name that Roc has passed on to me. I must say that it is very difficult to be combative when someone values you enough to refer to you as sweet. While Roc's late grandmother was one of the sweetest individuals I have ever encountered in life and differs remarkably from some of the clients I see, yet and still, my regard for these young girls is so high that I am willing to see something positive in them even before they show it to me. I did not understand the impact of my own words until a client stated that she didn't want anyone else to take her place as the "sweet girl." I promptly reminded her that I only see sweet girls so she should take comfort in the fact that she is surrounded by many just like her based on her connection to me.

I have no idea whether or not it is paradoxical confusion or what, but my clients and kids in general seem stunned when I interrupt another adult eager to express all of the negative things that the child has done and I instead give a compliment or question him or her about an interest or a special talent. Even the other adult is taken aback by my sincere interest in the young person. This is by no means scripted. I honestly care for children and the easiest way to present oneself as an alley is to like someone. Pleasant words will undoubtedly follow. Parents are usually confused when I suggest that they say something nice to their wayward children. They may wonder "how can this stranger expect me to say nice things about this kid who steals my car?" They think that it is easier for me because I have no real emotional investment when I initially meet a client. I am a parent myself so I do know that it takes time to be able to speak pleasant words through unpleasant situations, yet I must also admit that like the chicken or the egg scenario, it is important to question which came first; the poor behavior, or the lack of kind words. More likely than not, in the absence of the other four steps and kind words, negative behavior started to take root. This handbook once again is not to blame the parents, but to empower parents to realize that we as adults CAN win our children in the battle against the juvenile justice system. If we understand our strength, we can use it, rather than harsh words and physical violence to provide our children with their emotional and social needs.

I recall a situation in which a teenager stole money from his mother's purse. She was furious by his actions, yet she stated "he's a respectful boy so I don't understand why he would do something like this." I wanted to pause time, stand up and clap for her. Even in her frustration, she pointed out a positive characteristic in him and questioned the irony of his behavior when measured against his positive quality. Not only did this facilitate an emotional dialogue between them, but his self esteem was not deflated. So many parents tell me that positive words cannot be more effective than a good ole' spanking. I beg to differ. If I had a dollar for every time I have heard a parent tell me that their kids were immune to physical punishment, I promise you I would be wealthy! Hearing positive affirmations does something for the self esteem that no amount of spankings can. When a parent speaks positive words over their children, something happens deep inside of that child. I don't know if it is shock on the part of the child that someone is speaking positive words over him or her, or a sincere desire to meet the expectation of those words, but this technique works when it is done consistently.

In the case of Al, a very angry young man, I insisted on pointing out his positive attributes. I verbalized his positive qualities and expressed my expectations for him, based on his qualities. For instance, I never expressed an expectation for him to be anything other than what he was. That would be too overwhelming for him. Instead, I studied him in great detail in order for my verbalizations to be based on his strengths, in an effort to add more muscle to his strengths. Although on paper, he had a relatively low I.Q., he was insightful. I pointed this out to him quite often. Here he was, a sixteen year old that most adults feared because of his physical make up and violent history, but I instead focused on his insight. He never saw fear in me and he never heard doubt from me. I cannot help any child, if they do not possess the belief that I can…somewhere deep within. To foster that belief, my words must marry my actions. Considering I felt he had insight, I relied on him as the expert of his own life and offered positive reinforcement when he exhibited insight. I was not using my words to lie to him, I honestly found something positive about him and I highlighted it verbally. If I can find positive things to say about a child or teenager that I have recently met, I see no reason why a parent or teacher cannot do the same for a child or teen that they know so well.

I have consulted with several parents and teachers who suggest that some children are simply out of control. I do not view any child beyond help. Although there are perhaps those that exist, I have yet to meet a child upon introduction who cursed me out or physically assaulted me. I do not give children and teenagers a chance to dislike me because I like them instantly. I would not serve in this capacity if I did not like children. I know that it may seem difficult to find something positive about a child who is acting out, but as adults, before a child acts out against said adult, it is imperative to beat them to the punch and decide to like them, regardless of collateral reports that suggest misbehavior. Although I can readily read a chart on a kid or listen to an overwhelmed parent or teacher tell me about the kid, I formulate my own conclusions, based on the child himself rather than what others think of him. That is a lazy habit to develop; to rely on the opinion of someone else rather than develop a meaningful relationship with a child based on mutual respect. When a parent or teacher has a problem with a child, I ask them to reflect on how they treated and spoke to the child initially. Most adults put on the imaginary halo and recall several positive attempts to reach a "bad child." If we are honest, we will find that upon seeing behavior that we did not like or even relying on the opinions of others, we treat children and teens according to what we believe they are, rather than what they could be. The halo effect simply makes us feel warm and fuzzy inside.

One year at my daughter's school, there was a certain young man who I quickly gathered was the trouble maker in the classroom. He acted out for the teacher and the other students, but ironically he responded quite differently with my daughter. I watched her interaction with him and listened to her words. Although I imagine this boy had been a tyrant in the past, she spoke to him with positive words. In turn, he was respectful towards her. He was still angry, but even in his anger he managed to show her respect. I cannot stress the number of times that angry teens and even parents have cursed out my colleagues and others around me and actually have taken the time to apologize to me because I was a witness of the behavior. Why would that be so? I constantly sow positive words into others and they appreciate and remember that. Is that an easy task? Actually it can be once it is realized that all individuals have the potential to do good.

If I show a liking for a child or teen in the beginning, it is unlikely that I will be privy to the behavior that the young person exhibits among those who seek to control him or her. I try to help parents understand that one cannot truly control another, even if you gave them life. When parents control themselves, their children can follow suit and manage their own behavior. Even children who comply with their parents' expectations do not do so because they are being controlled. They have found safety in adhering to the rules and regulations that have been set forth by parents. When children do not follow expectations of their parents it is perhaps because they are not confident in the parent's ability to lead. I know this is a bold statement.

In the case of Al, he reasoned that because his mother could not handle her own life, as evidenced by her poor choices and her frequent contradictory statements, he should not follow her lead. Children listen to the things that we say even when we are not speaking to them so it is important that we monitor what comes from our mouths. This mother went from one extreme to the next in describing her son. One minute, he was her "gift" and the next he was her "curse." These verbalizations confused the young boy who came to see his mother's words as a puzzle with a missing piece that would never be found. Had she processed her own paradoxical feelings in her own individual time and used positive words with her son, she may have built a different relationship with him. I am not suggesting that parents should never express frustration, but frustration that sounds like hatred is counterproductive.

For the young girl who engaged in antisocial activities, it would be wise to suggest the following, "You are a valuable member of this family so I don't understand why you insist on keeping yourself a part from us," as opposed to "Why are you so stupid?" This was an actual response from a parent whose daughter frequently ran away from home. Telling her that she is valuable lessens her resistance and although she may give a sarcastic response, it is up to the parent to keep his or her cool. The "why are you so stupid" response is provocation for an altercation and in the case of family aggression and violence, there are no winners.

As a parent, I have nothing to prove with my children. They are aware that I pay the bills and take care of their livelihood so I don't feel a need to go toe to toe with them. If they are sarcastic with me, I promptly and firmly question them on their choices of words and redirect them to more appropriate language, but I don't waste a lot of time going to battle with them. I take the higher road as the responsible adult, let them know that I value them and then suggest that they help me understand why their actions are not consistent with the positive qualities that they possess.

There is a big debate among some of my colleagues concerning the battle between praise versus encouragement. I have seen and even written treatment plans (in the past) that suggest the clinician, parent, and teacher should offer praise, but in my honest opinion, I now believe that encouragement should be offered instead. If our goal is to raise circus acts then praise works here, because they are always performing for us. Whether they excel or not is based on what we think of them. To encourage is a quite different experience. So many clients are initially confused when they ask my opinion of something they have done and I in turn ask them what they think about it. I ask their opinion because their choices and behavior should not rely on what I think. Of course, I encourage young people to make adaptive choices, but I do not praise them when they make those choices, I simply encourage them to continue those behaviors if they enjoy the feeling of accomplishment that they receive.

I learned early on as a parent to not tell my children that I am proud of them for something that they have done. I am proud of them simply for being Amaris, Aria, Anais, and Aliya. They do not have to do anything special for me to sow positive affirmations into them. While I may experience joy each time they make honor roll, this is no different from the joy that I feel when someone in the store remarks on how well behaved they are. My children do not have to perform for me to like them and say nice things about them. Likewise, neither do my clients.

I recall two families that I saw on the same day. This was a strange experience because the two parenting styles were so very different. One parent had three children who were all disobedient for the most part. They had been adopted and had many issues that developed in their formative years within the confines of foster care. The other parent, also an adoptive mother had three children, whose problems seemed to be more of self esteem issues instead of behavioral problems. The former mother swiftly took counsel and used positive words when communicating to her children. Although she did not understand their behavior, which at times I must admit was rather bizarre, she was willing to consistently engage in positive communication with them. If she did use derogatory language towards them she did not do it in my presence and this was never reported. She understood the power of her words, so she used positive language with them even when they expressed inappropriate verbalizations.

I honestly don't think I have ever met a more patient individual. While her children's behaviors may have been quite irritating at times, they eventually learned how to self regulate their behaviors. They learned how to express themselves appropriately because they had a positive model to follow. While their behavior (upon the last time that I checked) did not represent angelic dispositions, they had never experienced any legal interaction because their mother focused on instructing them towards socially responsible behavior. In this case, like many others, this was no easy walk in the park. The mother was called at work, had to participate in several conferences with the teachers, and lost many nights of sleep, but she did not lose her children to the department of juvenile justice because she decided that this would not be an option for them.

In the case of the other mother, all of her children eventually entered the juvenile justice system and subsequently the adult jail system. None of them committed any major crime, but somehow it worked out that way. One too many domestic violence calls led the authorities to believe that the kids' problem behaviors could be better addressed within the juvenile detention centers. The latter mother did not hold back. She expressed herself fully without taking into the account the negative impact it would have on the children. She rarely made positive statements about or to the children who already suffered from extremely deflated self esteem. As a result, they saw no use in their lives (as their lives were within the home) so they subjected themselves to negative choices. What is sad about this story is that the mother has yet to realize that it did not have to be this way. One of the children still remains in DJJ and the others have matriculated to involvement with the adult legal system because their once minor violations evolved into a life of crime. I am not stating that the mother caused them to be incarcerated but her lack of positive engagement on their behalf did contribute to their fate.

Parents must understand and take seriously the fact that children get their own internal and external dialogues from the scripts that they are exposed to. If you don't believe me, listen to a four or five year old play house. Whether or not the child acts out a positive or negative parent and child relationship speaks volumes on how they view their own relationships with their parents and other relationships that they are exposed to. It was in listening to my daughter play "school" that I came to realize that her teacher was not a very friendly person. My daughter was only in the pre-kindergarten program for one month before we withdrew her and started to homeschool her. Her teacher later admitted to us in casual conversation that she did not like children so when she explained that our daughter was manipulating facts about her character a couple of days later, her explanation fell on deaf ears. Just as I believe that there are great therapists in the world, I also believe that there are great parents and teachers who are honestly trying to develop socially adjusted, positive individuals. I would be fooling myself however, if I believed that there were not those who could care less about the social and emotional development of children. While I will never understand why an individual would go through the labor of bringing forth a child into the world (as in the case of parenting) or take a job specializing in the educational development or therapeutic care of a child (school teacher, child therapist) when he or she had no intention of serving this population in a positive manner.

In a former school of my children, I would often walk down the hallways and I would be privy to information about various students. I don't know if the teachers thought I could not hear them or they simply did not care, but they obviously never took a class on privacy. They casually discussed the behavioral difficulties of various students and just as I heard these statements, I am certain that some of the children, even the subjects of these conversations heard them as well. What is a child to do when a teacher or parent openly expresses dislike for him or her? To the child this is a no-brainer; continue to act up and do so in an even more aggressive manner. The self-fulfilling prophecy is very real here.

I sat in on a conference in which teacher and parent went back and forth on how difficult a certain child was, in the presence of the child! After awaking myself from the shock of such foolishness, I excused the child from the conference in an effort to point out to them their own weakness in the situation. Here they were, two adults openly admitting that they were fragile in handling an elementary school student. Although the purpose of this exchange was to express frustration, what it did to the child was to further deflate his self esteem, considering they spoke about him as if he were not there. In addition, in an odd way it gave him power in the situation. He realized that his behavior had both of these adult women baffled so he reasoned that he now had power. Upon further investigation, it was revealed to me that his initial desire was to gain attention so the fact that he was able to stump both of them to the point in which a conference had to be held to explore their failed tactics in addressing his behaviors, he realized that he had secured attention. The attention was negative, but of course that did not matter.

Although I have years on them and a couple of degrees which bare my name on my office wall, I must admit like the teacher and the parent in the aforementioned example, I am stumped by my children sometimes. During these times, I quietly consult my husband and my mother, Shirley, who offers me insight based on fifty years plus of parenting. While I admit to my children that I am human and capable of making mistakes, I do not inform them that their behavior has gotten the best of me. That is for me to process through on my own time. It serves no point to inform my children that their behavior is overwhelming for me. It is my job as a parent to decipher why it is overwhelming in an effort to effectively address it.

I recall a situation in which I sat in the waiting room at a juvenile facility. It is not uncommon to witness frustrated parents, mostly mothers, who make a scene because of their disgust with their children's behavior. On this particular day, there were three mothers who were sitting there; two were discussing the negative behaviors of their children. One commented that her child was so far beyond her control that she was considering turning her custody over to the state. Another mother explained that her son used the "law" to justify his actions because he was made aware of his rights, through listening to the conversations between his mother and various police officers (who were called out to the home when he acted out). The mother who bragged about considering releasing parental rights because "wrap around, IFI, and all the other services don't help," quickly responded indicating that she NEVER spoke in the company of her daughter. Mind you, this was fifteen minutes after she had explained in great detail that she had had enough of her negative behavior. I watched the child as she sat there, taking in her mother's words that could be heard well beyond the place where she sat. The last mother never spoke, but she nodded in agreement. The mother with the son said something that stuck out in my mind. She said that "he's smart, he knows that all I'mma do is call the police and they will bring him back up here." I wanted so very badly to pull her aside and help her understand what her son was saying to her. He knew that his mother would not address his issues; she would call the police instead of dealing with him herself.

She saw his statement as being sarcastic (and rightfully so) but I also saw that it was rooted in a loud cry for help. He was confident that she would not address his issues, although she made it a point to declare to the other mothers that she calls the police each time he misbehaves. There was a time when calls to the police were reserved for reporting crimes, not as a means of controlling children. When I walked out of the room, I saw her son standing in the hallway. He looked down until I spoke to him. I don't remember exactly what I said, but I talked to him about the weather because it was nearing springtime. I do remember suggesting that he tie his shoe, as not to fall and I left him by saying "I hope things get better." He said "me too" in a hushed voice. It is very possible that he controlled the family through misbehavior, but I approached him on a level playing ground. The sound of his mother's voice in the next room became mere background noise. I can only imagine what life was like for him when such dialogue was a part of daily life.

As I conclude this chapter on the importance of using "tasteful words to speak life" over our children, I must include wisdom from my mother. I recall for as long as I have been surrounded by kids as an authority figure, which was possibly at the age of seven when I became an aunt, my mother has reiterated the importance of refraining from calling children "bad." I rejected this notion as a young person because I reasoned that I knew plenty of "bad kids."

As I got older, I continued to hold onto my belief that the word "bad" was not a four letter word. The real "no-no" were actions that came with such a definition for a child. As long as I was careful not to exclude children because they were bad, calling them bad would not do much harm. I rationalized that most bad kids had some idea that they were bad anyway. I proposed, it is not what one says, but how they mean it based on their subsequent actions. Calling a child bad, did less damage than treating the child as if they were bad. I coined the phrase "how I treat a child will determine how I treat him or her (therapeutically). All of that psychological rhetoric aside, my mother was right. The self fulfilling prophesy theory is very much real.

When a child or teen constantly hears negative verbalizations (whether it is warranted or not based on behaviors), he or she begins to define oneself by those verbalizations. If a child or teen feels negative already, the verbalizations serve as a form of confirmation for those mistaken beliefs. They are mistaken beliefs because as my mother stated there are no bad children, only poor choices. If a child or teen is met with positive verbalizations, he or she is then forced to reconsider the negative description that he or she originally held.

Parents should know more than children and teachers are trained to teach them, so the child reasons that the verbalizations from the parent and teacher must be legitimate. I actually had a client who stated to me "maybe I am wrong about myself since you think I am not bad, cause you have a license." I don't brag about my educational accomplishments, but if they can be used to encourage a child or teen to think in another way about oneself then I am all for it. I remember a child used the word "bad" to describe himself. I asked "who told you, you were bad," and he quickly remarked "everybody!" I followed up with "I do not believe you are bad," and he reminded me that I had just met him. I smiled and stated "yes, so now you can help me prove my theory about you as truth." Because I do not choose to see kids as most adults in their lives, I do not speak to them in the same language. As a result, my interactions are typically very positive.

Speaking tasteful words may take some getting used to for the parent and teacher who want respect based on the fact that he or she is an adult. I do not feel my adulthood or authority is threatened when I make the first move to sow positive words into the life of a child or teen who may be craving for that type of positive attention. I ask parents to take an inventory of all of the words that probably need to leave their household vocabulary and take notice of the changes when these words are replaced by words of encouragement and positivity.

In my family of origin, my mother stressed the need to remove "stupid" and "hate" from our vocabulary, and Roc and I have similar expectations in our family. This may take some time. Rearranging one's vocabulary does not happen overnight, but it is well worth the effort to use tasteful words when communicating to and about one's children. I once met a child who was detained when I completed an assessment for her. She shyly admitted that she didn't remember receiving a compliment from either of her parents until she was detained. When I asked what the compliment was, she looked down for a bit then squarely looked me in my face and stated "she (referring to her mother) said you look cute in your jumpsuit!" I looked at this 15-year-old baby in her juvenile justice furnished attire and I almost felt a tear. I can only imagine the true impact of her mother's words.

6

Bonus: Common Sense

Now that I have explained how children and teens can be provided with their need to be heard, supported, understood, appreciated, and validated, I must explore the 6th sense…..common sense. Some argue that common sense may not be so common, but from the frame of reference of social interest, common sense is our shared sense of knowledge.

When I meet a parent/parents and child, I make it clear that the family is its own expert. Once we get that out of the way, everything else just works somehow. All members of a family have both individual and collective desires and goals. Some initial goals may be unrealistic for the good of the family unit, but for every maladaptive goal, there is a useful one as well. The family, once empowered will eventually seek to reach useful goals because they will understand the benefit of doing so. My job is to facilitate an environment in order to expose the useful goals to the family. I do not rely on my clinical expertise to tell them what is right for them; instead I use it to help them discover that they hold the answer to their own health.

The best way for me to effectively share my thoughts on the use of common sense in addressing children is to provide examples. In a certain case of Tommy, there was a question as to whether or not he was psychotic or not. Some may disagree with me, but this is based on my clinical experience, which by no means is representative of everyone's story. Considering I chose to author this handbook, we will focus on my experience only.

As with the rest of the book, take what you will and the rest may empower someone else who needs it. Tommy had acted out and was referred for a 10-13 (involuntary hospitalization). While I do have some responsible friends in the school system and those who work as social workers, I have found that in the setting of school and other arenas, the 10-13 is overused. While there are some cases of psychosis, I have personally been privy to several situations in which the only mind in which psychosis existed was in that of the adult who suggested it. Within the juvenile justice system, it is routine for offenders to be evaluated and it is no surprise that psychologists are met with resistance and undesirable behavior. Imagine the stress that a parent feels when he or she is informed that the juvenile offender has a diagnosis in addition to offending behavior.

Tommy was angry. He was not psychotic. At times angry behavior is a part of psychotic behavior, but just as all Great Danes are dogs, but all dogs are not Great Danes; all psychotic behavior is socially abnormal but some socially abnormal activities (extreme anger) is not indicative of psychosis. I must add that when a child sits in a hospital room, waiting to be taken to yet another facility to be stabilized, irritability and agitation sets in. Add personality differences and some perceived defiance from the child or teen and you have a perfect situation to witness a child or teen act out. Once the child does this, it confirms what the school and hospital suspected….psychosis.

I cannot stress how many times I have had to argue with individuals (who have met my clients once) about a client's mental stability. While I did receive an A- in my grad school Abnormal Psychology course, I do believe I have a firm understanding of what the behavior looks like. I am just careful not to allow my own creativity to give life to something that is not there. By no means do I believe that I am invincible, but 911 is not on my speed dial. Before I label something as a crisis in which crisis stabilization is needed by way of a 10-13 (which once again is the formal name given to a situation in which an individual is "committed" to a mental facility or hospital for stabilization in Georgia), I try using what I have mastered, given my Masters degree….counseling.

As long as I can de-escalate a child, we do not have a crisis. Now I would not put my hand into the mouth of a hungry crocodile, but as of yet (and I knock on wood, though I am not superstitious) I have not come in contact with a client that I could not de-escalate. In some cases, the de-escalation takes some time, skill, and effort, but that's what I get paid to do. If it were always peaches and crème, everyone would always have dessert!

The common sense message that I am trying to convey in Tommy's case is that considering we as adult naturally hold the power, it is quite unfair to use our position and authority to define behavior as psychotic simply because we cannot figure it out (or at least we do not want to take the time and effort to do so). In the case of Michael, he was already involved with the juvenile justice system when it was suggested that there was an imperative need for me to apply for residential treatment for him. During this time, I was in charge of overseeing a program that was designed to be a last stop before residential placement.

Many may assume that it is arrogance on my part in believing that I can de-escalate all children, but it is my love for counseling that leads me to that conclusion. Some opt to subscribe to the belief that "you can't save em' all," because having such beliefs does not allow one to be set up for failure. I believe that the minute I believe that I cannot help a child, adolescent or family, I have failed them. My form of treatment works because I believe it does! When I respectfully declined to apply for residential placement for Michael, I was met with opposition. Here's a novel idea, let's try to identify the problem and figure it out before we take such drastic measures. Ignoring my counseling skills is like the chef with all of the great recipes who never cooks…out of fear. That is not my style. I love people too much to give up on them prematurely (or at all for that matter).

I hope you see where I am going with this common sense stuff. We have minds that are designed to gather, store, and conceptualize data and I believe that it is important to utilize that when addressing the needs of our youth. To categorically label them as monsters is a deadly game to play and I am not a killer. In the case of John, his mother was doing everything that she could in order to address his needs, but like so many other parents, her methods were ineffective because she did not know what those needs were. If parents want answers, they must know the questions. One cannot solve a problem with a missing piece of data….the problem can only be simplified. I once explained it to John's mom, as I have to so many parents; a "good" parent may honestly and earnestly attempt to help his or her child in life, but if the parent is working on problems A, B and C and the kid is suffering from problems L, M, N, O, P…there is a disconnect. The parent has to learn to bridge the gap between that disconnect. I believe in good parenting just like I believe in good counseling so I know that parents who were not originally in the same book as their children can ultimately make their way to the same page as their children. This can happen without losing one's child to the juvenile justice system.

Sometimes parents rely heavily on "the system" for answers and they find themselves agitated, upset, and betrayed because "the system" does not always have the best interest of the family in mind. How can they when they don't even know the family? I am certain you would find it amazing that I have so many clients who are asked questions by yours truly that no one else has ever thought to ask them before. Some examples include asking the kid who is obviously depressed "what makes him sad," questioning the runaway about what or who he is running from, or even asking a kid how long he has been having his particular symptoms. I find it odd that there are specific criteria designed to help diagnose an individual, but sometimes these criteria are not even taken into account before making a formal diagnosis and deciding exactly what to do with a kid. This is not only unethical to say the least, but it is not a common sense practice.

Tyler was a fourteen year old who ran away from home and his mother assured me under no uncertain terms that he was "outta control" and "couldn't be saved." The strange twist is, he was literally running from a step-father who had been sexually molesting him for years. The truth eventually came out and ironically his mother chose to remain with the step-father....it's no wonder why Tyler never decided to "run" back home!

Parents always ask me what they should do when their kid is already headed down the wrong path and I say to them "do whatever you can to get them down the right path." That may sound vague, but I think parents hold the answers to their own parenting questions, they just may need some support in achieving their goals. I often hear parents talking about the difficulty in raising children because children have so many rights. Children, like all other people SHOULD have rights. I think stories about children abusing those rights and calling 911 on their parents is a bit exaggerated like some urban legend that has been passed down from person to person. I empower parents not to live in fear. There are not any laws that state that parents cannot discipline their kids. The laws prohibit abuse and when a parent disciplines out of love as opposed to anger, there should be no room for abuse anyway. Child abuse (outside of having a naturally abusive parent) usually happens when an otherwise in control parent loses control and goes too far. These are the parents who may lose custody or even guardianship of their children. Parents who discipline with love, but firmness understand that structure is afforded to their children. Children need structure and cannot effectively thrive without it. There are several ways to exhibit a disciplined parenting style and excessive force and punishment is not the way.

We don't really believe in traditional punishment, because I have found that punishment is punishment not only for the child but for the parent as well. I encourage parents to use what I call "sitcom interventions" for punishment. This technique or series of techniques require creativity on the part of the parent. These are great, but unfortunately, you have to wait for the next handbook for those! I will tell you this though, we truly teach our kids lessons in the manner in which we address their behavior and problems in a memorable way to say the least. We can readily punish them, but in punishment, there is seldom a connection between the behavior and the punishment that is used. While some may argue that through classical conditioning, a child can learn that a spanking is connected to acting out, there are so many other lessons that a child can learn in such a situation. Furthermore, children are not dogs and while I appreciate my psychological forefather's great experiment, I must state additional details. Children also learn lessons about fear and limitations through spankings. We also teach children that violence is reasonable when we do not get desired behavior from others. These lessons certainly may not be the intention of the parent, but yet and still they can be learned.

I have never wanted my children to fear me....mutual respect is quite enough. If children learn to comply with rules and regulations out of fear alone then they lose the importance of exhibiting pro-social behavior. I never explain to my children that why they are to strive towards useful living or pro-social behavior is because "I said so." If they do things to please me only either they will cease to exhibit pro-social behavior in my absence or they will develop the need to be people pleasers. At either end of the spectrum this can become quite a detrimental character flaw. When I homeschooled my children I never said "1 + 1=2." I actually put it in real world, experiential, and tangible terms so they could have an appreciation for life and the way that it works. The same holds true with stressing the need for respect rather than fear.

Limiting oneself is another negative lesson that children learn from spankings. If a child is acting out and could possibly hurt himself, it seems to me that it makes more sense to simply redirect him or her rather than make a scene through force. Children learn and express themselves in different ways. I know of so many expressive children who may be viewed as troublemakers because they are not understood. Tammy was 14 by the time that I met her, but her problems started in kindergarten when she excelled at the top of her class. She developed a habit of speaking out of turn and to combat this behavior, she received many spankings. She would stop talking in short spurts, but ultimately she continued. She developed a reputation at her elementary school as a trouble maker and by the time she entered middle school, she hated school and earned herself a truancy charge. She did not get the true intended connection between the excessive talking and her spankings. What she did develop though was a general hatred for school. She started to limit herself. I have a talkative daughter who is also exceptionally smart and instead of using the same approach as Tammy's mother, I understand that my daughter's boredom is causing her to develop a loquacious communication pattern. Before her behavior becomes disruptive it is up to me to challenge her through supplementary work at home and to express my concerns to the teacher. I am careful not to suggest how the teacher oversees her classroom, but I also make sure that all of my kids' teachers know that Roc and I stress education. Once again, I believe in the home-school partnership (so much that I serve on the Governing board at their school).

What more suitable way to teach children that violence is a viable option to control others, than through the long time favorite….the spanking? I am not suggesting that all parents abandon spankings, but I do believe that parents should abandon spankings of excessive force and anger. This is probably abuse and it should not be ceased simply because of the threat of 911, it should be halted because of the long term concern for the child(ren) involved.

As an independent, social interest filmmaker myself, I am well aware that the film world gets a great deal of criticism about various violent movies, yet some of the violence that kids experience in their own homes make violent movies look like a romantic comedy. When spankings are the only way that parents redirect a kid from poor behavior, the kid will be prone to developing the idea that violence solves problems. We all know how true that is. So why do so many parents rely on spankings alone? Simple, it has been an acceptable form of discipline throughout the years, but honestly are the kids who were spanked (to make them more productive citizens) doing any better than the kids who were not spanked, in that same juvenile detention center? Catch my drift? If spankings could prevent all negative behavior from occurring, why hasn't it? Sometimes we use the excuse of "if kids didn't have so much power to call 911 and parents could spank openly, there wouldn't be so many people in prisons." I beg to differ. During my lifetime I have witnessed the evolution of this "power" that some speak of as far as children being empowered to call 911. Strangely enough if we believe this theory, the prison system was already flooded before parents lost their power (if having the power to abuse was power in the first place). Trust me, and I say this with the utmost sincerity, "knocking a child out" will not solve the problem. It will create an even greater disconnect between parent and child (and a lot of hospital bills)!

In dealing with families, I have learned to build bridges. Some may naturally think that that is the end of the story, but actually it is the beginning for me. Some therapists believe that if the bridge is built, families will naturally come….I take it a step further, I am willing to go over to their side (understanding life as they perceive it), grab hold of their hand (utilizing unconditional positive regard) and walk them over with me (guiding). This is what I have chosen to do, 24 hours, 7 days a week, 365 days a year as a therapist and supervisor out in the field. I charge you to do the same as parents. Build a bridge through communication, walk over to take that child's hand and hold it for dear life as you walk across the bridge together….parent and child….free (literally) of the juvenile justice system.

ABOUT THE AUTHOR

Kirsten Person-Ramey is a Doctoral-level, licensed professional counselor, originally from Atlanta, Georgia. In addition to teaching, speaking, and supervising other clinicians, she also sees children and families within their homes all over the state. As a mother of four daughters, Dr. Kirsten is interested in strengthening parent-child bonds and has developed several workshops to teach parents how to learn to speak the language of young people. In addition to therapy, Dr. Kirsten also co-owns a film production company with her husband, Roc that she uses to empower audiences through inspiring the human spirit, through independent social interest projects.

www.ingramcontent.com/pod-product-compliance
Lightning Source LLC
Chambersburg PA
CBHW070556170426
43201CB00012B/1861